THINKING LIKE JESUS

A Practical Guide to Encountering the Words and Wisdom of Jesus

Benny & Wendy Perez

Foreword by Judah Smith

Thinking Like Jesus: A Practial Guide to Encountering the Words and Wisdom of Jesus | Copyright © 2022 by Benny Perez and Wendy Perez

Manuscript prepared by Celina Mina (createwithcelina.com)

First printing 2022
Cataloging – in – Publication data available

ISBN 978-1-7339893-2-9 (international trade paperback)

Published with help from 100X Publishing

To our kids—Benjamin, Bella, and Benaiah.
May we give you our best, Jesus.

CONTENTS

Don't copy the behavior and customs of this world, but let God transform you into a new person by changing the way you think. Then you will learn to know God's will for you, which is good and pleasing and perfect.

Romans 12:2 NLT

Foreword

by Judah Smith

No pressure writing a foreword for my favorite (and only) sister and brother-in-law, right? We've now traversed more of our lives as adult family members than as children. We have raised children of our own. We have built communities of faith. We have grown and changed, at times disagreed, and have faced heartbreaking tragedy and exuberant triumph. But the end game has always remained the same—to bring people closer to Jesus Christ.

Thinking Like Jesus: A Practical Guide to Encountering the Words and Wisdom of Jesus is a testament to the lives of two individuals who said "yes." "Yes" through the good and the bad; "yes" when they wanted to say "no"; "yes" when it was inconvenient; "yes" when it was uncomfortable. That "yes" began with a "yes" in their hearts and minds—a willingness to exchange their own thinking with what Jesus would think.

We can often focus on a person's behavior and actions without considering the thoughts that ultimately led them down that path in the first place. Yet the Bible is clear: "For as he thinks in his heart, so *is* he" (Proverbs 23:7 NKJV). It's what takes place in our hearts and minds that determines the words of our mouths, the actions of our hands, and the direction of our feet. Indeed, the condition of your thought-life creates the condition of your daily life.

As you read through these chapters and take the time to prayerfully respond to the reflection questions, may you begin to experience a transformation in your thinking that ultimately transforms your life. After all, if we are truly Jesus-followers, then it makes sense that we should desire to think like Him in order to live like Him.

God bless you,
Judah Smith

think·ing | \ ˈthiŋ-kiŋ \ noun

Definition of thinking

1 : the action of using one's mind to produce thoughts
2a : opinion, judgment
2b : thought that is characteristic (as of a period, group, or person)

\ ˈthiŋk \ transitive verb

Definition of think

1 : to form or have in the mind
2 : to have as an intention

Chapter 1

We Have the Mind of Jesus

Your mind is incredible. To this day, neuroscientists continue to discover new things about the human mind and the capacity of the human brain. Did you know that every event you have experienced in your life so far has been recorded in your mind? That's every experience, every emotion, every joy, every trauma, and everything you have ever seen and heard. While you may not consciously remember it all, you can guarantee that it's all stored in your mind. All that accumulated, stored information creates the perceptions through which you filter future events. The mind contains our past. Our history. And if we do not have the revelation that as followers of Jesus, we have the mind of Jesus, we can end up repeating our history. We can become stuck in life and feel like the same things keep happening over and over again.

When we become a follower of Jesus, the Bible teaches that we become "born again." What is imperative to understand is that not only is our spirit regenerated, but we are actually given a new mind by God. This is significant because we all have areas in our lives that we are wanting to see changed. People typically believe that internal change will take place when external change takes place. So, they wait for circumstances to change because the world operates with an "outside-in" perspective. However, the Kingdom of God operates with an "inside-out" perspective! Having the mind of Jesus means that we can experience a change of mind first, which ultimately brings change to our actions.

The Apostle Paul writes that we are now spiritually alive in Jesus and that we have not just been given new life, but we have been given a new mind:

No one can know a person's thoughts except that person's own spirit, and no one can know God's thoughts except God's own Spirit.
And we have received God's Spirit (not the world's spirit), so we can know the wonderful things God has freely given us. When we tell you these things, we do not use words that come from human wisdom. Instead, we speak words given to us by the Spirit, using the Spirit's words to explain spiritual truths. But people who aren't spiritual can't receive these truths from God's Spirit. It all sounds foolish to them and they can't understand it, for only those who are spiritual can understand what the Spirit means. Those who are spiritual can evaluate all things, but they themselves cannot be evaluated by others. For,
"Who can know the LORD's thoughts?
Who knows enough to teach him?"
But we understand these things, for **we have the mind of Christ.**

1 Corinthians 2:11-16 NLT (emphasis added)

We have the mind of Jesus! This means that we don't have to live thinking and concluding the way we did before we came to Jesus. Let me simplify it even more: If Jesus doesn't think it, I don't have to think it.

The human brain fascinates me. I have spent a lot of time reading about the brain and how our mind works. Throughout this chapter, I will be drawing upon some of the key things I have studied.[1] Neuroscientists refer to the brain as the last great frontier. So much of what we believed about the brain just a few years ago has been proven to be no longer true at all. For example, it was believed that parts of the brain damaged through a stroke or a trauma could never recover. Since then, it has been proven that recovery is possible due to what can now be seen through new ways of scanning the brain.

(In this book, we have included space for you to take notes.)

_____

_____

_____

_____

_____

_____

_____

Indeed, the brain is an incredible organ. But I'm not just focusing on your physical brain—I'm interested in your mind, your thoughts, and how they relate to your perception of life. "Neuroplasticity" is your brain's ability to change. However, it doesn't change on its own. It needs stimulation and your thoughts—what you choose to dwell on—play a significant role in this. "Neurogenesis" is the process by which new neurons are formed in the brain. Your brain is continually growing new brain cells. It was once believed that we only had a specific number of cells, which decreased as we got older, causing many of the issues

---

[1] I encourage you to explore the range of resources by Dr. Caroline Leaf (https://drleaf.com/)

associated with aging. Science has since uncovered something astonishing: A brain that loses brain cells is a brain that is not thinking the right way. Both neuroplasticity and neurogenesis show a connection between the health of our brain and the health of our thoughts.

As a follower of Jesus, this excites me! It reminds me of the Apostle Paul's words of encouragement to the church at Philippi:

And now, dear brothers and sisters, one final thing. Fix your thoughts on what is true, and honorable, and right, and pure, and lovely, and admirable. Think about things that are excellent and worthy of praise.

Philippians 4:8 NLT

Here's the verse again in another version:

So keep your thoughts continually fixed on all that is authentic and real, honorable and admirable, beautiful and respectful, pure and holy, merciful and kind. And fasten your thoughts on every glorious work of God, praising him always.

Philippians 4:8 TPT

The New King James Version of this verse uses the word "meditate" instead of "think about." These thoughts are not fleeting thoughts! We are to intentionally think deeply about the right things. But that's easier said than done, right?

Three challenges of the mind

Have you ever driven your car somewhere, pulled up and parked, and suddenly realized that you didn't remember any part of the journey? You were driving on autopilot, distracted by other thoughts going on in your mind. Perhaps you've experienced reading a book and suddenly realized that you have simply been reading the same sentence over and over again. Once again, you were distracted, not focused.

Neuroscientists claim that distractibility is one of three major challenges of the mind. A study conducted in the United States of America revealed that 47% of US American adults don't pay attention to what they are doing.[2] They live their lives distracted the majority of the time! Social media can be a wonderful tool, but it has quickly become one of our generation's key distractions.

Our household recently experienced a problem. We bought some indoor plants from a gardening store without knowing they had fruit flies. I soon discovered them while working at my computer one evening. Have you ever seen a fruit fly? They are tiny! Yet, the smallest of flies had the power to distract me from what I was trying to focus on. They had no ability to hurt me, only the ability to distract me. What are some of the small things that we are allowing to distract us?

A second major challenge of the mind is loneliness. According to a poll, 76% of middle-aged US Americans said they suffer from high levels of

---

[2] Matthew A. Killingsworth, Daniel T. Gilbert, "A Wandering Mind Is an Unhappy Mind", Science 330, no. 6006 (2010): 932

loneliness.[3] I love that science supports what the Word of God teaches us about the need for community. A lack of genuine and authentic fellowship can cause significant mental health challenges. This is something that the COVID-19 pandemic lockdowns and restrictions revealed to us all. While technology means we are more connected than ever before, it also causes us to feel more disconnected than ever before due to the lack of authenticity. Being seen, known, and loved for who you genuinely are is an innate need in all of us.

A third major challenge of the mind is negative self-talk and a lack of purpose. So many have negative beliefs about their worth and value. They have no clear sense of direction, and life feels meaningless. Depression, anxiety, and suicide are on the rise globally, and while there are many complex reasons for this, it is clear that negativity and hopelessness are major contributors.

Distractibility. Loneliness. Negativity and lacking purpose. These challenges bombard our minds; as followers of Jesus, we must intentionally make decisions about how we think and what we dwell on. We have the mind of Jesus!

---

[3] Ellen E. Lee, Colin Depp, Barton W. Palmer, Danielle Glorioso, Rebecca Daly, Jinyuan Liu, Xin M. Tu, Ho-Cheol Kim, Peri Tarr, Yasunori Yamada and Dilip V. Jeste, "High prevalence and adverse effects of loneliness in community-dwelling adults across the lifespan: role of women as a protective factor", International Psychogeriatrics 31, no. 10 (2019): 1447

A Jesus Mentality

What does it actually mean to have the mind of Jesus? It's about perceiving life as Jesus did. It's about filtering life experiences and perceptions through His Word. Do you remember those armbands that were popular several decades ago? The ones that had WWJD? on them? What would Jesus do? Well, having the mind of Jesus means asking, "What Would Jesus THINK About This?"

Having the mind of Jesus is looking at life from the viewpoint, values, and desires of Jesus. We choose to not entertain any thought in our minds that God doesn't have in His mind about us. In other words, if it's not in the Father's head towards me, it should not be in my head towards myself! When we read the Scripture, we need to explore how Jesus thought, not just what He did. We need to understand His mentality.

1. Jesus understood that He was unconditionally loved and valued by His Father.

Jesus knew that the Father loved and accepted Him unconditionally. If that's the way He looks at Jesus, that's the way He looks at you. As Jesus is, so are we in this world (see 1 John 4:17). The Father's love wasn't based on good or bad behavior; your behavior doesn't qualify God's love for you either! In fact, Romans 5:8 says, "But Christ proved God's passionate love for us by dying in our place while we were still LOST and UNGODLY" (TPT, emphasis added). Before we could DO anything, Jesus DID everything for us.

2. Jesus' identity was fixed on what His Father said, not what other people said.

Jesus was so grounded in His identity. It was shaped by His Father's words. In the book of Matthew, we read the account of the baptism of

11

Jesus (see Matthew 3:13-17). At this point, Jesus has not performed any miracles yet; He has not accomplished anything spectacular. However, when He gets baptized and comes out of the water, the Bible says that the Heavens opened, the Holy Spirit descended upon Jesus like a dove, and God the Father said, "This is the Son I love, and my greatest delight is in Him" (Matthew 3:17 TPT).

Before Jesus did anything, His Father affirmed His identity. When we live with the mind of Jesus, we secure our identity to what God the Father says about us and discard the opinions of others. One of my favorite quotes is, "God's opinion of you makes man's opinion irrelevant."

3. *Jesus believed the best in His followers.*

The mentality of Jesus was to believe the best in His disciples and see their potential. He believed the best in Peter even though He knew Peter was going to deny Him. He believed the best in Thomas even when He knew Thomas was going to doubt Him. Jesus even chose a disciple that would betray Him. I don't know about you, but this completely goes against my nature. Unfortunately, our human nature quickly defaults to suspicion. Imagine what our lives would be and feel like if we chose to believe the best in people? That even if we may disagree with someone, we still also see the potential within them. Jesus could see the best in others because His identity was secure. One of the biggest hurdles to believing the best about others is first believing the best about yourself. If you have a hard time believing the best about others, do you believe you are unconditionally loved and accepted by God?

4. *Jesus' mind was set on fulfilling God's will, not His own.*

Jesus came to earth to fulfill the will of His Father. He didn't do anything unless His Father told Him to do it (see John 5:19). Proverbs 16:1 says, "Go ahead and make all the plans you want, but it's the Lord who will ultimately directs your steps" (TPT). What would happen if we embraced the mind of Jesus and took on this mentality? What if we actually submitted our plans to God and trusted His ways instead of our own? How would your life change if you got out of bed each morning and said, "I have the mind of Jesus. Today, I'm choosing to trust God's way for my life"?

_____

_____

_____

_____

_____

_____

_____

5. *Jesus didn't give up His eternal perspective over temporary pain.*

As Jesus hung on the cross, He cried out, "My God, my God, why have you forsaken me?" (see Matthew 27:46). He truly understood great pain and suffering. Yet, in the midst of great distress, He did not give up when He had to suffer shame and die on a cross. He knew of the joy that would later be His (see Hebrews 12:2). The imagery in Hebrews 12 is so powerful. It was like a never-ending slideshow of faces was in front of Jesus. When His body was wracked with pain and His soul was in agony, He saw you, He saw me, and that hope is what sustained Him. Whatever we may be going through right now is temporary. We have an eternal hope that we must hold on to! We live with the perspective of heaven.

6. *Jesus' obedience came out of security, not fear of retribution.*

Jesus obeyed the Father in all seasons—not out of fear of retribution, but out of security. He was secure in the Father's love. "For God will never give you the spirit of fear, but the Holy Spirit who gives you mighty power, love, and self-control" (2 Timothy 1:7 TPT). Fear is not from God. Therefore, the mind of Jesus is not motivated by it. We do not obey God because we fear punishment; we obey God because we have a relationship with Him, and we trust Him. We obey because we have been empowered through the Holy Spirit with mighty power, love, and self-control.

7. *Jesus never thought lack; He always thought abundance.*

Jesus never filtered things through the lens of lack. He thought about things through the perspective of abundance. The reason why we easily think that a problem is big is because we think about what is lacking or how we are lacking. While Jesus never denied a problem, He recognized that His Father was bigger than the problem. He knew the abundance that is found in our Heavenly Father. One of the most beautiful names of God is *Jireh*, our provider. Christianity is not the denial of challenging or painful circumstances. It is a proclamation of someone who is greater than the challenge.

8. *Jesus knew that all things are possible.*

Jesus never doubted the power and provision of His Father. When we face difficulty and times of crisis, we tend to be overwhelmed by how impossible things seem. We ask ourselves, "How on earth is this going to work out?" But that question is not ours to figure out! We need to stop praying prayers that we can figure out and start praying prayers that only God can figure out. It's usually too big for us anyway! Why are we wasting our time trying to figure it all out?

9. *Jesus thought of endings as beginnings.*

Perhaps you are in the middle of transition right now. How did Jesus think about transition? Jesus considered endings as necessary. We think that endings are final, but Jesus looked at endings as new beginnings. I have come to realize that my life must have the necessary endings in order to enter into new seasons and even new relationships. Jesus said it best in John 12:24. "Let me make this clear: A single grain of wheat will never be more than a single grain of wheat unless it drops into the ground and dies. Because then it sprouts and produces a great harvest of wheat—all because one grain died" (TPT). Jesus was framing His own death in light of a new beginning—the new covenant!

10. *Jesus knew that truth would always prevail.*

Jesus didn't argue about the truth because He knew the truth would prevail in the end. He is the truth, after all! He didn't attempt to prove that He was the Son of God. He didn't reveal things prematurely; instead, He trusted in His Father's timing. When we take on the mind of Jesus, we don't need to enter into debates that want to prove one person right and one person wrong. We don't even have to defend Jesus. Just as Jesus died and rose again, the truth may be buried for a season, but at the right time, it will come to light again.

Having the mind of Jesus means that we now look at life the way Jesus looked at life. We perceive life the way Jesus perceived life, and we know how God the Father looks at us because that's the way He looked at

Jesus. However, we also have a part to play in this. This is our responsibility: If we've been given the mind of Jesus and we believe the mind of Jesus, we now need to put the mind of Jesus into action in our lives by applying the way Jesus thinks to our own thoughts and circumstances.

There is a process. For the remainder of this chapter, I want to share four actions that have helped me do this: Reject every lie, renew my mind, replace old thoughts, and release the right words.

Reject every lie

The first thing I must do to take on the mind of Jesus is to reject every lie. It is not God's responsibility to reject the lies in my thinking; it is my responsibility to reject them. A lie is the only weapon that the enemy actually has against us. God's Word, the Bible, is known as truth. Whatever thoughts in your mind that don't line up with the truth of God's Word must be rejected. Why? Because if you believe a lie as truth, it will affect you as if it were true. If we believe a lie as truth, it will now act like it is true.

Your immune system contains white cells that can identify "foreign invaders" such as a virus. The white cells' job is to reject that virus and fight against it. Isn't it incredible that your body is wired to reject the wrong things? Likewise, having the mind of Jesus means rejecting the wrong thoughts! I mentioned earlier that the enemy's main weapon is the lies he tells us. Jesus describes the enemy as being "a murderer right from the start! He never stood with the truth, for he's full of nothing but lies—lying is his native tongue. He is a master of deception and the father of lies!" (John 8:44b TPT). Jesus identifies that lies come from the enemy whenever the enemy opens up his mouth. He is a liar. However, if a lie is told continually, people usually end up accepting it as truth.

16

During World War II, Adolf Hitler once said, "If you tell a big enough lie and tell it frequently enough, it will be believed." The enemy only has one ability: to lie. If we do not reject and fight it, over time, we can end up believing it. So, how do we actually reject a lie?

You cannot reject something until you identify it. Let that sink in. You cannot reject what you do not identify. We need to be honest and talk about our thoughts. Throughout the Psalms, David continually pours out his heart to the Lord. To be honest, I used to read the Psalms and say, "Wow, David's got some issues." Then I realized something—he was just being authentic and real. Can I ask you a question? Who are you really honest with? Do you have people in your life that you can go to and honestly share the thoughts that are going through your mind? Which people help you identify the lies so that you can reject them? That's the power of community. We need the authentic relationships of other honest followers of Jesus who can tell you the truth, without condemnation or shock, and say, "You're not thinking right!"

The Bible teaches us that:

...the weapons of our warfare *are* not carnal but mighty in God for pulling down strongholds, casting down arguments and every high thing that exalts itself against the knowledge of God, bringing every thought into captivity to the obedience of Jesus...

2 Corinthians 10:4-5 NKJV

You can't pull something down overnight. You pull it down brick by brick; you pull it down little by little. You keep pulling it down, and what was once so big begins to get smaller and smaller. Jesus is always into steps. He is always into moments that make up a process. I still believe that God can do instant miracles. Absolutely. However, as followers of Jesus, taking on the mind of Jesus is a daily process. Real change takes place daily. We choose to reject lies daily!

_____

_____

_____

_____

_____

_____

_____

_____

Renew my mind

After identifying and rejecting the lie, we need to renew our mind. In the book of Romans, Paul writes to people living in a very corrupt culture, encouraging them to not take on the thinking of their environment.

Don't copy the behavior and customs of this world, but let God transform you into a new person by changing the way you think. Then you will learn to know God's will for you, which is good and pleasing and perfect.

Romans 12:2 NLT

Notice that it does not say, "let God transform you into a new person by changing your circumstances or actions." The enemy wants you to believe that the state of your mind depends on the state of your circumstances. However, having a new mind is not tied to circumstances; it's connected to what you are thinking about. When you begin to have a transformed mind, you will begin to have a transformed life. Right believing leads to right living. Your life changes in the direction of your thoughts. Transformation is an interesting word because transformation indicates, again, a process.

Each day, I remind myself that I am becoming all that God has already declared me to be. I am the righteousness of God in Jesus. I can't get more righteous; I can't get more Holy. As I begin to believe what God has declared me to be, my thinking transforms. And as my mind is renewed, my life begins to transform and line up with what God has already declared me to be.

Now, transformation is messy. It's not straightforward. However, legalism wants to clean up the mess prematurely because legalism is more concerned about appearance than transformation. Legalism is more concerned about getting your behavior right, but if your mind isn't renewed, it's just a matter of time before your behavior goes back to how it once was.

The Greek word for transformation is *metamorphosis*. It is associated with a caterpillar turning into a butterfly. You can't see what's going on in the cocoon, but I do know one thing—change is happening in that cocoon, and you'll kill the butterfly if you open up that cocoon prematurely. When you get serious about renewing your mind, you may need to cocoon yourself away from certain people for a season. You'll be able to reconnect when you learn to fly. A cocoon creates an environment where change can take place away from outside stimuli that could ruin what is happening. Renewing the mind is uncomfortable and requires hard work. But remember this: pain is not our preference, but it is part of the process.

Replace old thoughts

Replacing old thoughts may initially seem the same as renewing the mind. But this is different. This is the very practical step in taking on the mind of Jesus. This involves replacing every lie with the truth and finding a promise for every problem. For example, you may have identified the thought that says, "I have to handle a crisis on my own." Through renewing your mind, you realize that this is not how Jesus thinks. So, you now turn to the Word of God and find a verse and promise that replaces that incorrect thought. You begin to think to yourself, "My God will never leave me nor forsake me" (see Hebrews 13:5). Or how about this passage from a well-known Psalm:

Lord, even when your path takes me through the valley of deepest darkness, fear will never conquer me, for you already have! You remain close to me and lead me through it all the way. Your authority is my strength and my peace. The comfort of your love takes away my fear. I'll never be lonely, for you are near. You become my delicious feast even when my enemies dare to fight. You anoint me with the fragrance of your Holy Spirit; you give me all I can drink of you until my heart overflows. So why would I fear the future? For your goodness and love pursue me all the days of my life. Then afterward, when my life is through, I'll return to your glorious presence to be forever with you!

Psalm 23:4-6 TPT

Every lie has a truth, and every problem has a promise.

Throughout my years of leading and pastoring, I have had to turn to God's Word in order to replace lies with truth. I have had to intentionally choose to think new thoughts: "God is for me. God has plans for me. My future is in God's hands. I can trust God. He is working all things for good."

Release the right words

After identifying and rejecting lies, renewing the mind, and replacing old thoughts, it's time to release the right words. It's one thing to think something; it's another thing to declare it out loud. Suppose I asked you to start counting in your head from one to ten. You then get to the number five, and I suddenly tell you to say your name out loud. Do you know what would happen? The counting would stop in your mind as soon as you said your name out loud. Your brain must stop to listen to what your mouth is saying. What we often do, though, is just let our mind talk without saying anything back.

In times of financial uncertainty, my wife and I know that God is our provider. He is the provider of our family and our church. Circumstances do not change how we think. However, I have learned to declare these thoughts out loud: "Father, you take care of the birds, and you take care of the flowers. I thank you that you're going to take care of my family and the church. You have taken care of us in the past, and you will do it again." We must remind ourselves of God's faithfulness!

Embrace the process

We are all on this journey of taking on the mind of Jesus. It is a lifelong process, and there will be times of struggle. But I want to remind you that you do not do this in your own strength. We have the Holy Spirit who comforts and encourages us in times of distraction, loneliness, and despair. We are empowered by grace to do the hard work of rejecting the lies, renewing the mind, replacing old thoughts, and releasing the right words.

Reflection

1. Distractions, loneliness, negative self-talk, and lacking purpose are listed as some of the greatest challenges people face. How would you describe your greatest challenge in life right now? What currently consumes your mind the most?

_____

_____

_____

_____

_____

_____

2. Ten observations are made about Jesus' mentality:

- Jesus understood that He was unconditionally loved and valued by His Father.
- Jesus' identity was fixed on what His Father said, not what other people said.
- Jesus believed the best in His followers.
- Jesus' mind was set on fulfilling God's will, not His own.
- Jesus didn't give up His eternal perspective over temporary pain.
- Jesus' obedience came out of security, not fear of retribution.
- Jesus never thought lack; He always thought abundance.
- Jesus knew that all things are possible.
- Jesus thought of endings as beginnings.
- Jesus knew that truth would always prevail.

Which one stands out to you the most? Why? In what way(s) is the Holy Spirit wanting your mentality to change?

_____

_____

_____

_____

_____

3. List three things that you believe about yourself, which you know do not line up with the Word of God.

_____

_____

_____

_____

4. Now, turn to the Bible and find three verses, which replace the lies you have just listed. Write those verses down.

_____

_____

_____

_____

_____

_____

_____

_____

5. What prevents you from being honest with others about what you are truly thinking? What step can you take today to create or continue building authentic relationships in your life?

_____

_____

_____

_____

_____

_____

6. Write down a Bible-based, faith-filled declaration that you can say out loud every morning when you first wake up.

_____

_____

_____

_____

_____

_____

_____

Study verses:
1 Corinthians 2:11-16 NLT, Philippians 4:8, 2 Corinthians 10:4-5,
Romans 12:2, Psalm 23:4-6

Chapter 2

New Mind, New Words

Have you ever felt down but couldn't put your finger on what was making you feel that way? That happened to me recently. After a whole day of trying to work it out, I finally sat down and prayed, "Holy Spirit, why am I feeling what I'm feeling?" If only I had come to the Holy Spirit right away! As I started to think about what my thought-life had been like leading up to these feelings, a specific thought came to the surface. The thought surprised me. I knew right away that the thought was not from the mind of Jesus. Just like I discussed in the previous chapter, I chose to reject the lie and declared, "This thought is not of the mind of Jesus." My feelings didn't instantaneously change in the moment, but they soon changed.

You have been given the mind of Jesus, which also means you have been given new words to speak. Life is about what you are thinking about and what you are speaking out. The thoughts you think and the words you speak determine the course of your life. A new mind must lead to new words. Scripture teaches us that our thoughts determine who we are (see Proverbs 23:7) and what you say flows from what is in your heart (see Luke 6:45). Our lives are built upon how and what we think. If we want our lives to change, we cannot wait for circumstances to change. By God's grace, we must change our thinking.

We need to embrace the mind of Jesus! In other words, you should not have a thought in your mind towards yourself that God doesn't have in His mind towards you. You should not have a thought in your mind towards your life that God doesn't have in His mind towards you. I have learned to examine my thoughts by asking, "Is that the mind of Jesus?" If it isn't, I have to choose to let it go.

When we take on the mind of Jesus, we begin to see a change in the words we speak. The mind of Jesus gives us new perspectives and the revelation that God is the God of the new. We have a change of thinking, and our thinking now lines up with the Word of God. Right thinking results in right living. A new mind leads to a new life. We can try to begin change through our behaviors, but it's only a matter of time before we go back to our old ways because behavior is the result of beliefs.

In his letter to the church in Corinth, the Apostle Paul writes:

For it is Christ's love that fuels our passion and holds us tightly, because we are convinced that he has given his life for all of us. This means all died with him, so that those who live should no longer live self-absorbed lives but lives that are poured out for him—the one who died for us and now lives again. So, from now on, we refuse to evaluate people merely by their outward appearances. For that's how we once viewed the Anointed One, but no longer do we see him with limited human insight. Now, if anyone is enfolded into Christ, he has become an entirely new person. All that is related to the old order has vanished. Behold, everything is fresh and new. And God has made all things new, and reconciled us to himself, and given us the ministry of reconciling others to God.

2 Corinthians 5:14-18 TPT

In Jesus, we can look at the future with hope and expectation, not through eyes that are dim with disappointment and discouragement. In Jesus, we do not allow the current challenges in our lives to determine what we believe God is able to do in our lives. These verses teach us that if anyone is in Jesus, the old has gone, and everything has become new. However, to gain a deeper understanding of what this means, we need to further unpack the connection and contrast between Adam and Jesus.

_____

_____

_____

_____

_____

_____

_____

No longer in Adam but in Jesus

The Apostle Paul finds it necessary to remind the church of Corinth that they are now in Jesus, which means that there was once a time in which they were not in Jesus. Suppose you walked into a building. Once inside, you could confidently say that you were in the building. However, there was a time that you were not in the building; you were still in the parking lot! This is a simple analogy, but remember that being in Jesus is not a feeling; it's a position. We were not in Jesus at the start. We have come out from somewhere else. When we were not in Jesus, we were in Adam.

When we were born, we were born into the Adamic race—the human race.

The Bible teaches that we were separated from God. Because of sin, we were dead to God. Colossians 2:13 (TPT) clearly says, "This "realm of death" describes our former state, for we were held in sin's grasp. But now, we've been resurrected out of that "realm of death" never to return, for we are forever alive and forgiven of all our sins!" Christianity is not about once being bad and becoming good; it's about once being dead and becoming alive! "When Adam sinned, the entire world was affected. Sin entered human experience, and death was the result. And so death followed this sin, casting its shadow over all humanity, because all have sinned" (Romans 5:12 TPT).

When we put our faith and trust in Jesus, we go from being in Adam to being in Jesus. Adam was from the earth, Jesus was from heaven. Adam sinned; Jesus was sinless. Adam brought the curse; Jesus brought the blessing. Adam was initially put in charge of creation; Jesus is the King of new creation.

In other words, just as condemnation came upon all people through one transgression, so through one righteous act *of Jesus' sacrifice*, the perfect righteousness that makes us right with God and leads us to a victorious life is now available to all. One man's disobedience opened the door for all humanity to become sinners. So also one man's obedience opened the door for many to be made perfectly right with God and acceptable to him.

Romans 5:18-19 TPT

Think about it; Adam reached out and grabbed a fruit from the tree that caused humanity to fall, and yet Jesus allowed Himself to be nailed to a tree to redeem humanity! The old is gone; the new has come.

You are a new person

In Jesus, you belong to God's family. You are a son or daughter of God because of new birth, not because of worth. We were never worthy enough on our own. But now, we have a new heart, a new mind, and new desires. Our significance and identity are found in Jesus. He has brought you out of one kingdom and brought you into a new kingdom.

Your hearts can soar with joyful gratitude when you think of how God made you worthy to receive the glorious inheritance freely given to us by living in the light. He has rescued us completely from the tyrannical rule of darkness and has translated us into the kingdom realm of his beloved Son. For in the Son all our sins are canceled and we have the release of redemption through his very blood.

Colossians 1:12-14 TPT

Here is a question for you in light of this chapter so far: If your sins are canceled, why are you remembering them? If God forgets, why do you remember? I believe that we often forget the things that we need to remember and remember the things that we need to forget! That's the plan of the enemy. In Adam, you may have been an addict. In Adam, you may have been an alcoholic. In Adam, you may have been a liar. But in Jesus, you are a new person. Your sins are canceled, and you have been redeemed by His very blood.

The old has gone

I often have conversations with people who ask me what it means when the Apostle Paul writes that the old has gone. As a new person, your old way of thinking has gone. Your old way of believing has gone. Your old way of speaking about your life has gone. Before, you were in charge. Now, God is in charge. Before, you trusted in your own strength. Now, you trust in God's strength. Before, you relied on your own reasoning and ability. Now, you rely on God's supreme wisdom and power. In the old covenant, it was obedience that brought the blessing. The root was obedience, and the fruit was blessing. In the new covenant, the root is the blessing, and the fruit is obedience.

Times of challenge and crisis put all of this to the test. The year of 2020 and the COVID-19 pandemic has been difficult, painful, uncertain, and heartbreaking for us all. Indeed, I personally had to keep reminding myself that even in the midst of a pandemic, I am in Jesus, and I am a new person. I had to choose daily to take on the mind of Jesus and speak words in line with His Word. I had to let go of my own way and trust God in a whole new way. God is the God of the new, and we can believe that new things are on the way!

_____

_____

_____

_____

_____

_____

"What are the people saying about me?"

In the Gospel of Matthew, we read about Peter's revelation of Jesus. Jesus asks what appears to be a straightforward question, but in doing so, confronts the old and ushers in the new.

When Jesus came to Caesarea Philippi, he asked his disciples this question:
"What are the people saying about me, the Son of Man? Who do they believe I am?"
They answered, "Some are convinced you are John the Baptizer, others say you are Elijah reincarnated, or Jeremiah, or one of the prophets."
"But you—who do you say that I am?" Jesus asked.
Simon Peter spoke up and said, "You are the Anointed One, the Son of the living God!"
Jesus replied, "You are favored and privileged Simeon, son of Jonah! For you didn't discover this on your own, but my Father in heaven has supernaturally revealed it to you. I give you the name Peter, *a stone*. And this rock will be the bedrock foundation on which I will build my church—*my legislative assembly*, and the power of death will not be able to overpower it!

Matthew 16:13-18 TPT

Let me give you some background. Caesarea Philippi was a certain place in Israel known as being a pagan stronghold. Caesarea Philippi was known as a dark place; it was a place where pagan gods were worshipped, and evil practices took place. In the ancient world, it was believed that

33

this was none other than the gates of hell—Satan's stronghold. Let me put it this way—it was definitely not the type of place where the Jews of Jesus' day would choose to go to for a day trip! So, why does Jesus take His disciples to Caesarea Philippi? He brings His disciples there to break old mindsets and give them a new revelation of who He is, emphasizing that His mission is more powerful than that of the enemy. Let's unpack two things that happened to Peter as a result.

1. *Peter receives a brand-new thought.*

When Jesus asks the disciples who people think He is, they give Jesus old answers, referring to John the Baptist, Elijah, Jeremiah, and other prophets. However, Peter gives a completely different response: "You are the Anointed One, the Son of the living God!" This answer had never been given before; it was a new answer. Peter's response is so new and revolutionary that Jesus declares he could only have received this thought from God the Father.

If we are not careful, we can become too familiar with Jesus, meaning that we look at Jesus with old eyes based on past experiences. My prayer is that the Holy Spirit would pour out a fresh illumination of who Jesus is, just like Peter receives in this story. Peter's spiritual eyes are opened, and he sees Jesus as the fulfillment of what John the Baptist, Elijah, Jeremiah, and the prophets had pointed to all along. The old makes way for the new.

This story amazes me because Peter's revelation of Jesus takes place in what was known as a demonic location. They are standing at the "gates of hell," and he receives this new thought about Jesus! When you're going through pain and challenge is typically when you receive a new illumination of who God really is. The toughest times in my life are when I receive a fresh understanding of who Jesus really is.

2. *Peter receives a brand-new identity.*

Along with his new thought, Simon Peter receives a new name. The name Simon means 'reed'. A reed blows in the wind. If the wind blows left, reeds bend to the left. If the wind blows right, reeds bend to the right. However, the name Peter means 'stone', something solid and unmoving. When your mind is illuminated by heaven, not only do you see Jesus the way He truly is, but you see yourself the way you truly are. It is important to note that Peter receives this new identity even though Jesus knew Peter would deny Him three times in the months to come. Peter's identity was not determined by his behavior, actions, and mistakes. In fact, I imagine that when Peter did deny Jesus three times, knowing that Jesus had given him his new name despite his actions would have brought comfort and encouragement.

_____

_____

_____

_____

_____

_____

_____

It is so important that you listen to what Jesus calls you because there are many other things that seek to determine your identity. There are three things upon which you can base your identity if you are not actively taking on the mind of Jesus:

- What you have accomplished (the performance lie)
- What you have (the possession lie)
- What others think of you (the people lie)

Peter has a brand-new revelation about who Jesus is, which results in him receiving a brand-new revelation of himself.

The new words you speak build your life

Your words will build your life. Words are not just for communication; they are for creation. The very first time spoken words are recorded in the Bible is for creation (see Genesis 1:3). Your words have creative power. "Words kill, words give life; they're either poison or fruit—you choose" (Proverbs 18:21 MSG). Words create atmospheres, mindsets, and legacies. They create vision, dreams, and nightmares. We must be so careful with the choice of words we use as we can either build up or tear down somebody's life or our own.

I will never forget my eighth-grade teacher, Mrs. Sheldon. At that time, I was really struggling physically with sickness. She noticed that I was not doing well, and on more than one occasion, she would look me in the eye and say, "Benny, I don't know what God has for you, but I do know that you're going to change the world." At that time, I certainly did not feel like a world-changer. At that time, I never would have imagined what I am doing today with my life. Mrs. Sheldon is no longer alive, but her words are still living today through me.

The words you speak will either build you or bind you:

Then Jesus called to the crowd to come and hear. "Listen,"
he said, "and try to understand.
It's not what goes into your mouth that defiles you; you are defiled
by the words that come out of your mouth."
Then the disciples came to him and asked,
"Do you realize you offended the Pharisees by what you just said?"
Jesus replied, "Every plant not planted by my heavenly Father will
be uprooted, so ignore them.
They are blind guides leading the blind, and if one blind person
guides another, they will both fall into a ditch."
Then Peter said to Jesus, "Explain to us the parable that says
people aren't defiled by what they eat."
"Don't you understand yet?" Jesus asked. "Anything you eat passes
through the stomach and then goes into the sewer. But the words
you speak come from the heart—that's what defiles you. For from
the heart come evil thoughts,
murder, adultery, all sexual immorality, theft, lying, and slander.
These are what defile you. Eating with unwashed hands will never
defile you."

Matthew 15:10-20 NLT

Jesus' point is clear: If I embrace the mind of Jesus, my words will be the evidence of this.

Live in the new

As we conclude this chapter, here are three things that I believe with help you put this into practice:

1. *Filter what you take in.*

Just because it's on TV doesn't mean that you should be watching and listening to it. Just because it's on social media doesn't mean you have to like and share it. If the beliefs and thoughts being shared do not line up with the mind of Jesus, reject it. Stop accepting words into your life that can contaminate your spirit and mind. Filter what you take in.

2. *Focus on the new perspective.*

Most of the time, we cannot change our circumstances. If you can, of course, you should! But when you cannot change your circumstances, what you can do is change your perspective. Look at how far God has brought you. Think about the good things in your life. Take time to say thank you and be grateful for what is going right.

3. *Fearlessly declare who you are in Jesus and keep moving forward.*

In one of his letters, I believe Peter, nearing the end of his life, reflects on the new identity he received from Jesus and now tells all followers of Jesus:

But you are God's chosen treasure—priests who are kings, a spiritual "nation" set apart as God's devoted ones. He called you out of darkness to experience his marvelous light, and now he claims you as his very own. He did this so that you would broadcast his glorious wonders *throughout the world.* For at one time you were not God's people, but now you are. At one time you

knew nothing of God's mercy, because you hadn't received it yet,
but now you are drenched with it!

1 Peter 2:9-10 TPT

Write it down. Memorize it. Tape it to your wall. Make it your lock screen. Whatever you have to do to keep it in front of you until you internalize who you really are!

Reflection

1. In your own words, describe what it means to no longer be in Adam but in Jesus.

_____

_____

_____

_____

_____

2. Who is Jesus to you right now?

_____

_____

_____

_____

3. Three identity lies are mentioned in this chapter:

• The performance lie
• The possession lie
• The people lie

What is the Holy Spirit revealing to you about how you measure your value and worth?

_____

_____

_____

4. Are there words that have been spoken over you in the past that you know are negatively affecting you today? The Holy Spirit can empower you to forgive the person who said those words. Write a prayer in which you express your decision to forgive and ask the Lord to heal you from the impact of those words.

_____

_____

_____

_____

_____

_____

_____

_____

_____

5. When it comes to filtering the words you take in on a daily basis, is there anything you need to start saying "yes" to or "no" to?

_____

_____

_____

_____

_____

_____

_____

6. Read the following passage of Scripture slowly and out loud. Underline the key words or phrases that stand out to you the most.

But you are God's chosen treasure—priests who are kings, a spiritual "nation" set apart as God's devoted ones. He called you out of darkness to experience his marvelous light, and now he claims you as his very own. He did this so that you would broadcast his glorious wonders *throughout the world.* For at one time you were not God's people, but now you are. At one time you knew nothing of God's mercy, because you hadn't received it yet, but now you are drenched with it!

1 Peter 2:9-10 TPT

Study verses:
2 Corinthians 5:14-18, Matthew 16:13-18, Proverbs 18:21, Matthew 15:10-20, 1 Peter 2:9-10

Chapter 3

Jesus Thinks Process

On one occasion, Jesus was preaching to a crowd on the shore of Lake Galilee. A vast multitude of people was pushing to get close to Jesus to hear the word of God. He noticed two fishing boats at the water's edge, with the fishermen nearby, rinsing their nets. Jesus climbed into the boat belonging to Simon Peter and said to him, "Let me use your boat. Push it off a short distance away from the shore so I can speak to the crowd."
Jesus sat down and taught the people from the boat. When he had finished, he said to Peter, "Now row out to deep water to cast your nets and you will have a great catch."
"Master," Peter replied, "we've just come back from fishing all night and didn't catch a thing. But if you insist, we'll go out again and let down our nets because of your word."
When they pulled up their nets, they were shocked to see a huge catch of fish, and their nets were ready to burst! They waved to their business partners in the other boat for help. They ended up completely filling both boats with fish until they began to sink! When Simon Peter saw this *astonishing miracle*, he knelt at Jesus' feet and begged him,
"Go away from me, Master, for I am a sinful man!"

Simon Peter and the other fishermen—including his fishing partners, Jacob and John, the sons of Zebedee—were awestruck over the miracle catch of fish.

Jesus answered, "Do not yield to your fear, Simon Peter. From now on, you will catch men for salvation!" After pulling their boats to the shore, they left everything behind and followed Jesus.

Luke 5:1-11 TPT

We think instant; Jesus thinks process

We live in an "instant gratification" culture, don't we? Our culture loves the credit card and the fad diet; we want items and results, and we want them now! We often don't want to do the hard work or have the self-control and patience to obtain what we want. I have recently been in a growth season of shifting from a "consumer mindset" to an "investment mindset." To be honest, it's been challenging! There's a phrase that states, "No pain, no gain"—my motto stated, "No pain, no pain." Humor aside, I realized that if I wanted to see lasting positive change in my health, I needed to commit to a process. But that is so hard when I crave instant results. We think instant, but Jesus thinks process. We only see our current circumstances, but Jesus sees the end from the beginning. Our God sees all things through the perspective of eternity, and I believe that He takes us on a process in the present to prepare us for what's to come in the future.

The problem is that we often want to short-circuit the process and avoid seasons of growth. It's not fun! It hasn't been fun for me to start getting up earlier to head to the gym. It hasn't been fun to do that one more squat. It hasn't been fun to replace French fries with zucchini fries!

However, I want to encourage you to trust God, who knows the end from the beginning, to outwork that process in your life.

"Let me use your boat!"

This story of the miracle catch of fish is the first interaction and encounter that Peter has with Jesus. I personally think that Peter is one of the most well-known and relatable characters in the new testament. As a disciple, he is so honest and authentic and desperately wants to do things well for Jesus. However, Peter has his weaknesses, doubts, and failings. There is a process that he will need to embark upon, and it all begins the night Peter sets out to catch fish.

Imagine the scene. Peter is a fisherman by trade. He, along with other fishermen, have been out fishing all night, but they haven't caught a single fish. They would have been tired, discouraged, and in need of a meal and some rest. But first, they must clean their nets. Nearby, Jesus is preaching to a crowd of people. Many are trying to push their way through the crowd to get closer to Jesus to hear His words.

_____

_____

_____

_____

_____

_____

_____

It's at this point that Jesus walks on over to Peter's boat, hops in, and says, "Let me use your boat!" Let's pause here for a moment. There is something about this that I personally find interesting. The Bible was written under the inspiration of the Holy Spirit, but God used human beings to write the words. The Holy Spirit inspired them, but the words still reflected the writers' unique personalities. Luke, the writer of this Gospel, was a doctor. Doctors need to be detailed and are specific in what they record. This is true of Luke—every single detail that he writes down is for a specific purpose.

What I find interesting is that Luke does not record anything from the sermon that Jesus preaches to the crowd. We can assume that thousands of people were impacted that day by the teachings of Jesus. Yet, Luke writes about none of this. Instead, he only chooses to record the words spoken between Jesus and a fisherman by the name of Simon Peter.

The request to use the boat does not seem significant in that moment. In fact, for Peter, it may have seemed like more of an inconvenient request, especially after a long night of hard work! In our own lives as followers of Jesus, it can be easy to ignore the seemingly insignificant leadings of the Holy Spirit. We can go to church and get excited by a brilliant sermon. And then the Holy Spirit asks, "Would you open up your home and start a small group?" We can go to a prayer and worship night, strongly sensing the presence of God. And then the Holy Spirit says, "It's time for you to start tithing." A small group. Tithing. Doesn't sound flashy or glamorous. But neither did the words "let me use your boat."

The truth is that instant gratification isn't a recent concept. It started in the very beginning—in the book of Genesis. Eve is tempted to eat the forbidden fruit, thinking she will become like God. Instant! The desire to want everything right away is a human condition. We always want something for nothing. We always want a shortcut. We always want to get out of pain. We don't want to have to walk through it. However, I want to remind you that we do not endure seasons of growth like people who have no hope. Our hope is not in our government or our economy. Our hope is not in our bank accounts or job titles. Our hope is Jesus. And when Jesus asks to use your boat, you can be sure that what seems insignificant is about to turn into something significant.

Jesus is always doing something

Let's continue on with the story. Jesus now sits in Peter's boat and continues preaching to the crowd. From what takes place later in the story, we can assume that Peter is now also in the boat. Jesus talks, and Peter sits there, perhaps feeling idle.

I have sometimes felt this way in the middle of working through a process with God. Perhaps you can identify. God asks you to do something, you do it, and now it feels like nothing else is happening—like you're in a holding pattern. However, Jesus, because of the very definition of who He is, cannot do nothing! He is a creator—even when He seems to be doing nothing, He is doing something. Peter thought he was just sitting idle in the boat. He had no understanding that he was in the midst of having his heart opened and softened. He had no idea that faith was growing in his heart. He had no idea that Jesus was about to extend an invitation that would change the course of his life forever.

In our own lives, we can find ourselves in seasons in which we feel idle. We cannot sense God at work in our lives. I want to encourage you to never despise the times where it seems like you are simply sitting. God is doing something on the inside of you. A process is taking place. He is always working in you! He is setting something up, but you need to allow time to make things clear. He is opening up doors through which you will walk in the seasons to come. He is orchestrating divine connections with other people who will play a part in your future. When we have no idea what God is doing, we must remember that He is always doing something. We cannot short-circuit the process.

"Cast your nets!"

As Jesus concludes His teaching, He turns to Peter and tells him to row into deep water and cast the nets, promising a great catch. Let me rephrase how these instructions from Jesus would have sounded to the ears of Peter: "Go and do the wrong thing at the wrong time in the wrong way." What Jesus was now asking Peter to do did not make any sense. Fishing took place at night, not during the day. The nets had already been cleaned. The fishermen were done and ready to go home!

We like to think that miracles suddenly happen out of nowhere. But when we reflect on the time and events leading up to a miracle, we realize that miracles don't happen in a vacuum. There is a process. Jesus didn't walk up to Peter out of the blue and tell him to go out and cast his nets. He first asked to use Peter's boat. If Peter had not given Jesus the boat, there would have been no great catch. The simple steps of a process are leading you towards miracles and breakthroughs!

Process begins in the night

While this story takes place in daylight, Peter's process started during the night. It was through the night that Peter worked hard yet caught nothing. It was through the night that his labor and toil were all in vain. It was through the night that Peter came to the end of himself. What Peter went through during the night set him up to receive Jesus' words in the daylight.

Faith comes by hearing the words of Jesus. In the middle of a night season, we need to live with the mind of Jesus and let our ears hear the words of Jesus. We declare words of faith by declaring what Jesus has said: "Jesus, you are who you say you are. You said you're my healer. You said you're my deliverer. You said you're my restorer. You said you're a miracle worker. You said you're my provider. You said you're my strength. You said you're my power. You said you're my sustainer. You said you're my banner. You said you will never forsake me. You said that you set a table even in the presence of my enemies. You said you're everything that I need!"

Somewhere between Jesus asking Peter to use his boat and telling Peter to cast his nets, faith was born. And that faith enabled Peter to act on the words of Jesus, resulting in the miraculous, abundant catch of fish. Do you know what fascinates me the most? We focus so much on wanting the miracle. However, when the miracle finally arrives, the miracle becomes irrelevant compared to the miracle worker. The greatest miracle in this story is the fishermen's encounter with Jesus. How do we know this? They leave behind the catch of fish to follow the One who had spoken into their lives. Peter now realized the power and the provision that was standing before him. Before this miracle, the boat and the net had represented Peter's power and provision. Now, he had encountered someone so much greater and was willing to lay it all down in order to follow Jesus. This is indicative of the process, which had been taking place the entire time— from the inside-out. Jesus knew what Peter would need for his future. The very water upon which Peter pushed out the boat, went out deep, and let down his nets was the very water upon which he would walk in the days to come. Likewise, Jesus knows what you will need for your future!

During the period of 2008 to 2010, our family experienced some of the most difficult and darkest years of our lives thus far. We wanted that season to end quickly, but year led to year. We desperately tried to come up for air, but wave after wave kept crashing upon us. It was excruciatingly painful. Somehow, by the grace of God, we made it through. He sustained us.

Over ten years later, in the midst of a pandemic and so much global upheaval and uncertainty, I can see that God knew back then the endurance, courage, and strength that we would need today. In the same way, right now is a season of growth—a process that is preparing you for what's to come. After all, He sees the end from the beginning.

_____

_____

_____

_____

_____

_____

As you continue the journey of living with the mind of Jesus, remember that Jesus does not think "instant"; He thinks "process." Perhaps you find yourself in the middle of the night. You are working so hard but have nothing to show for it. You're in the grind and survival mode. I believe you will experience Jesus as your sustainer and the lifter of your burdens during this part of the process. Perhaps you're like Peter, and Jesus is asking for your boat. It's time to take that step and give Him your time, your resources, your talents—whatever it is that is being asked of you. I believe you will experience Jesus as your peace during this part of the process. Perhaps you are feeling idle. You don't feel like anything is happening. I believe you will experience Jesus' faithfulness in this part of the process. Perhaps you are preparing to cast your nets, but it does not make sense. It seems like it's the wrong thing and the wrong time in the wrong way. I believe you will experience Jesus as a miracle worker in this part of the process.

Reflection

1. How do you feel when you have to wait for something?

_____

_____

_____

_____

2. Describe a season in your life in which you had to go through a long process. What lessons did you learn through that season?

_____

_____

_____

_____

_____

_____

3. Fill in the blank with what you believe the Lord is asking you to let Him use:

"Let me use your _____."

4. Is there an area in your life in which you feel nothing seems to be happening? How does knowing that this is part of the process change your perspective?

_____

_____

_____

_____

_____

5. Write a prayer below expressing your willingness to trust Jesus even when things don't make sense, and you're in the middle of a dark valley.

_____

_____

_____

_____

_____

_____

_____

_____

_____

_____

_____

_____

_____

_____

_____

_____

Study verses:
Luke 5:1-11, Romans 10:17

Chapter 4

Jesus Thinks Application

"Therefore everyone who hears these words of mine and puts them into practice is like a wise man who built his house on the rock. The rain came down, the streams rose, and the winds blew and beat against that house; yet it did not fall, because it had its foundation on the rock. But everyone who hears these words of mine and does not put them into practice is like a foolish man who built his house on sand. The rain came down, the streams rose, and the winds blew and beat against that house, and it fell with a great crash."

Matthew 7:24-27 NIV

We think information; Jesus thinks application

In addition to the instant gratification discussed in the previous chapter, I want to highlight that we also live in a culture that values knowledge and information. We are in the information age, right? We can get information with a tap on the screen and within a few moments of scrolling. If you want to learn something new, you can look it up so easily on one of the many devices that fill our homes. You can learn how to cook from Gordon Ramsay on TikTok. You can learn how to shoot better three-pointers in basketball from Stephen Curry on MasterClass. Indeed, we are not short of information. However, just as we think instant, but Jesus thinks process, we think information, but Jesus thinks application.

Information overloaded; application deficient

When we examine the life of Jesus, it is clear that He didn't just think a lot of things—He demonstrated it through His words and actions. Jesus didn't just teach information; He applied it throughout His own ministry on earth. Interestingly, Jesus was most frustrated by the Pharisees because, despite their vast wealth of Biblical knowledge, they did not apply it personally. They could quote Scripture but not put it into practice.

This story of the wise and foolish builders takes place following Jesus' well-known Sermon on the Mount (see Matthew 5 and 6). During the Sermon on the Mount, Jesus teaches a wealth of spiritual principles and introduces a whole new way of living life. I can imagine that my own mind would have felt overloaded from so much information! It is not a coincidence, therefore, that Jesus wraps things up with this story about two different men—one who builds his house on the rock and one who builds his house on sand. Jesus makes it clear that our application of His words makes all the difference, not just listening to them!

Decisions, not intentions, determine your foundation

There have been times in my own life that I have identified with the foolish man who built his house on sand. I have been to church, heard sermon after sermon, written down notes, listened to podcasts daily, completed Bible studies, and read inspiring Christian books. But it's all just remained as information in my mind. I never got around to actually applying it. I intended to but didn't. Perhaps you can relate to this also. This is what Jesus calls building your house on sand.

The Word of God is powerful, but it doesn't become transformational until we decide to obey it and put it into practice. If I were to ask you what the most spiritual thing is that you can do, you might respond with prayer or worship, or evangelism. These things are great, but they all start with another action—the act of deciding. I believe the most spiritual thing we can do on a daily basis is to decide. God has given us the gift of free will! He's given us the ability as human beings to choose. Before you pray, you first decide to pray. Before you worship, you first decide to worship. Before you share your faith, you first decide to start the conversation. And if we want to apply the Word of God, it must start with a decision—to shift from being a hearer of the Word to being a doer of the Word.

_____

_____

_____

_____

_____

_____

Let me share two reasons why it can be hard to apply God's Word.

1. *Applying God's Word takes work.*

In the Gospel according to Luke, this same story is also recorded but with some additional details. In Luke 6:48, the phrase "dug down deep and laid the foundation" (NIV) is used. The idea of building a house sounds exciting because we visualize the end result. The reality of building the house is hard work! Before we can ever move into that house, builders need to dig down deep and lay the foundation. It's messy, it's tiring, it seems never-ending.

Applying the Word of God is easy when you agree with it. Putting Scripture into practice is easy when it's something you already want to do anyway. Obeying the Bible feels exciting when circumstances are good, and all is going well in life. But God wants to mature us so that we still choose to apply His Word when life gets messy. When we don't fully understand His Word. When we really don't want to put it into practice. When obedience is going to require sacrifice.

I remember moving into our first house and feeling so excited about setting up each room and having our own yard. Until the IKEA boxes arrived and I had to assemble the furniture piece by piece. Until all the plants were delivered and I had to get up early and dig holes into the ground. Building sounds amazing, but it's really just hard work!

There are things that God is asking us to apply to our lives, which are hard. Forgiveness. Generosity. Tithing. Patience. Self-control. The shovel comes out, and we have to do the hard work of digging down deep. Thankfully, we have the Holy Spirit to help us. We do not do this hard work in our own strength. The grace of God not only covers our sins but empowers us to live the life that He has called us to live.

2. *Hearing God's Word can feel like enough.*

Let me explain this. Sometimes, we can hear the most incredible sermon and feel so inspired and exhilarated in the moment. We walk out of the service in such a good mood, believing that transformation has just taken place. Until we get to our car and can't find our car key. Until we reach for our iPhone to call for help and realize it's dead. Until we accidentally drop the iPhone and the screen cracks. The inspiration and exhilaration vanish! In fact, we no longer remember a single word of that incredible sermon.

It's in the space between hearing the Word and applying the Word that the enemy would like to distract, discourage, and deceive you. If we are not aware of this, we can have moments of feeling pumped up by the Word of God and believe that's all we need. This is deception. James 1:22 says, "Do not merely listen to the word, and so deceive yourselves. Do what it says" (NIV). Feeling good about the Word is not applying the Word. Simply feeling good about the Word will not enable us to experience the lasting results of actually taking the next step and applying it to our lives. The two houses may have looked the same from the outside, but the storm exposed the unseen foundation.

The great theologian, D.L. Moody, once said, "Our great problem is the problem of trafficking in unlived truth. We try to communicate what we have never experienced in our own life." Posting a Bible verse on social media is great and can make us feel good. But are we living out that verse? Telling a friend who is going through a tough time that we are praying for them can make us feel good in the moment. But do we actually take time to do it? Don't be deceived; hearing God's Word is not enough.

Hold up the mirror of freedom

Anyone who listens to the word but does not do what it says is like someone who looks at his face in a mirror and, after looking at himself, goes away and immediately forgets what he looks like. But

whoever looks intently into the perfect law that gives freedom, and
continues in it—not forgetting what they have heard, but doing
it—they will be blessed in what they do.

James 1:23-25 NIV

This metaphor given by James is an uncomfortable one, isn't it? It's uncomfortable because you know that in real life, you would never look in the mirror, see dirt on your face, and not wipe it away. And yet, this is exactly what we do spiritually speaking when we simply think information, not application. When you read the Word of God, it reads you. We are confronted by the standard of His Word and the condition of our own souls. It's uncomfortable to have the real state of how you're doing exposed. We want to keep that hidden. Like the foundation of the house that was built on sand.

_____

_____

_____

_____

_____

_____

_____

God wants to address things in our lives that need to change. However, application without a right relationship will turn into religious acts. God does not want to point things out to shame you. He is pointing these things out to grow you and turn you into the best version of yourself!

I want to encourage you that as you look into the mirror of God's Word—the perfect law—it will bring freedom. To be honest, there was a time when I did not equate God's Word with freedom; I equated it with not having fun. But when storms hit my life in the form of challenges and crises, I quickly saw the benefits of living a life of application. After the storm, my life still stood firm—secure, stable—on the rock. Freedom.

Living with the mind of Jesus is a process and requires application.

Reflection

1. How do you incorporate the Bible into your daily life?

_____

_____

_____

_____

_____

_____

2. Write down one thing that God is currently speaking to you about through His Word.

_____

_____

_____

_____

_____

3. What is one step you can take today to put God's Word into practice regarding what you have written above?

_____

_____

_____

_____

_____

4. What advice would you give to someone who is finding it difficult to apply something from the Bible to their own life?

_____

_____

_____

_____

_____

_____

_____

_____

_____

_____

_____

_____

_____

_____

Study verses:
Matthew 7:24-27, James 1:23-25, 1 Corinthians 2:16

Chapter 5

Jesus Thinks First Things First

When I was growing up, my parents expected me to contribute to the household. Even as a young kid, there were certain chores that were mine to do. Looking back, I appreciate the work ethic that my parents taught me—selfishness and entitlement were not a part of my childhood home! My main chore was to cut the lawn. Sounds simple enough, right? Let me give you some more details. It was a gigantic lawn. We had both a huge front yard and backyard. There was so much grass! Here's another important detail: I grew up in the era of the push lawnmower. No motor. I would spend hours and hours pushing the mower forward and pulling it back. Let's also not forget having to sharpen the blades on a regular basis. Some of you reading this probably have no idea what I'm talking about!

Due to how long it took, mowing the grass typically happened on Saturdays. I would wake up and hear the sounds of Saturday morning cartoons coming from the television. Just as I would get comfortable on the sofa and join in watching with my siblings, my parents would walk into the living room and say, "Benny, first things first. It's your job to mow the lawn. Once you get that done, you can enjoy the rest of your Saturday." First things first.

The power of priority

Throughout His ministry on earth, Jesus not only preached to the crowds; He made sure that He took time to teach His disciples. In the Gospel of Matthew, Jesus gathers His disciples and begins to teach them about Kingdom principles. I like to refer to the following passage of scripture as His "first things first" message:

"How could you worship two gods at the same time? You will have to hate one and love the other, or be devoted to one and despise the other. You can't worship the true God while enslaved to the god of money!"

"This is why I tell you to never be worried about your life, for all that you need will be provided, such as food, water, clothing— everything your body needs. Isn't there more to your life than a meal? Isn't your body more than clothing?

"Consider the birds—do you think they worry about their existence? They don't plant or reap or store up food, yet your heavenly Father provides them each with food. Aren't you much more valuable to your Father than they? So, which one of you by worrying could add anything to your life?

"And why would you worry about your clothing? Look at all the beautiful flowers of the field. They don't work or toil, and yet not even Solomon in all his splendor was robed in beauty like one of these! So if God has clothed the meadow with hay, which is here for such a short time and then dried up and burned, won't he provide for you the clothes you need—you of little faith?

"So then, forsake your worries! Why would you say, 'What will we eat?' or 'What will we drink?' or 'What will we wear?' For that is what the unbelievers chase after. Doesn't your heavenly Father already know the things your bodies require?

"So above all, constantly seek after the realm of God's kingdom and the righteousness that proceeds from him, then all these less important things will be given to you abundantly. Refuse to worry about tomorrow, but deal with each challenge that comes your way, one day at a time. Tomorrow will take care of itself."

Matthew 6:24-34 TPT

Jesus is sharing His thoughts on what our priorities should be. Just as He illuminated the disciples' thinking, He desires us to think like Him. And a vital part of living with the mind of Jesus is having the same priorities, which are highlighted in these verses.

Our focus is on God the Father

Jesus begins by stating that His disciples cannot have more than one master. He recognizes that the weighing concern and pressure of having enough resources and possessions can easily become a master. However, Jesus says that our priority is to focus on our Heavenly Father—our provider—not on the provision we may need. As we focus on Him, these other things will be taken care of.

Unfortunately, I have heard many preachers use these verses to proclaim that money is bad—that you cannot be truly spiritual if you have a lot of money and that poverty is a virtue to obtain. This is not the mind of Jesus. Jesus teaches that you cannot serve money, but money can serve you. Jesus teaches that though our focus is not on money, it does not mean that we cannot have it. Money is not bad, nor is it something to avoid; money is a tool to be used for the glory and the honor of God. In other words, if you are blessed financially, you do not need to hide it or apologize for it. Use your God-given abilities to create wealth to be a blessing to others!

We must always return to the singular priority of our Heavenly Father. When we think "His will first," it puts all the other distractions of our life into perspective, whether it's a trial or an amazing opportunity. What does God think about it? What is God's plan for my life? Even if the job seems like it's everything I've ever wanted, or I just know the person I'm dating has to be "the one." What does God think about it? This is the application of our priorities as we think more and more like Jesus.

By faith is how we live

Throughout this passage, Jesus questions why we worry and tells us that we should not worry. In other words, we are to live by faith. What is living by faith? Trusting that God will take care of what we need when we need it. Which means trusting He is who He says He is. Our provider. Our hope. Our salvation. Our healer. Our restorer. Our peace. This is counterintuitive because society drills into us the need to see it before we believe it. However, God's Kingdom is about believing before we see it. When we focus on God, faith begins to grow and produces fruit in our life. I am not telling you that you are to do nothing—to quit your job and just wait for money to fall down from the sky. No! We are to be good stewards of what is in our hands to do right now and trust God to provide and make a way.

Thinking like Jesus means living a life of adventure. That's a good way to frame it, isn't it? It often involves taking steps of faith without necessarily understanding the whole picture but choosing to obey anyway. Culture is a paradox. It admires successful risk-takers while promoting safe, comfortable, and risk-averse lifestyles. By risk, I do not mean foolishness. I mean steps of faith in which you know you have heard from God and have sought out wise counsel.

_____

_____

_____

_____

_____

_____

Many years ago, when Wendy and I told Wendy's parents, Wendell and Gini Smith, that we had decided to move to Las Vegas, the first question they asked us was, "Do you have a word? Has God clearly given you a word about this from Scripture?" When we assured him that we did have a clear word, they replied with, "Well, this is going to be hard for us to see you move, but if God has told you to do this, you need to obey Him. You need to step out and live by faith."

All these years later, Wendy and I are seeing the fruit of taking that step of faith. We had no idea that we would plant a church. We had no idea that it would grow to thousands of people. But God knew. Understanding is overrated, and obedience is underrated. What is waiting for you on the other side of your obedient faith step?

Look at the examples

Jesus always chose examples that were relatable to those listening to Him teach. When He asked His disciples to look at the birds and the flowers, He was using these as relatable examples of the faithfulness of God. In our context, looking up at the birds flying in the air or gazing out at fields filled with flowers may not mean much to us. But I believe we all have our "birds" and "flowers." We all have our examples that we can look at when we need to be reminded of the faithfulness of God.

I remember in 2008, in the middle of the Great Recession, we were going to lose our church building. We had been given forty days by the bank to close on a modified loan they had proposed, but we were short several million dollars. It actually was a win on our behalf, but on the other hand, it was insurmountable. We had been given the opportunity to modify our loan but had no feasible means of acquiring that amount of money. I still remember the moment I received a phone call from a couple who did not attend our church and who also did not live in our nation. They said, "We heard you are in trouble." I had never met them before in my life, and God miraculously used them to allow us to rescue our church property. That's my "birds" and "flowers!"

You need to make your list; a list that reminds you of that time when you had barely any money in your bank account, yet somehow, the rent still got paid. A list that reminds you of the day a bag of groceries turned up at your doorstep. A list that reminds you of that seemingly impossible situation that was resolved at the very last minute. A list that reminds you of that evening when an unexpected person gave you a miracle gift, which was exactly what you needed. I know what my birds and flowers are. What are your birds and flowers?

Seek first the Kingdom

My Sunday school teacher taught me Matthew 6:33, which has been my life verse ever since I was that little boy mowing the lawn: "But seek first the kingdom of God and his righteousness, and all these things will be added to you" (ESV). It's not enough to just say don't do something. It's not enough to say, "Don't think like that" or "Don't worry about that," We also must replace that thought, worry or action. If we don't replace it, we actually become fixated on not doing it and inevitably end up doing it again because it's all we were focused on! Jesus is giving us this invaluable lesson right here; it's not enough to say, "Don't worry about what you will eat or wear." He gives us the objects of our attention: His Kingdom and His righteousness.

Why does Jesus make such a radical statement? He doesn't want us to ignore our worries and anxieties; He wants us to combat them by giving us this promise. He realizes that in this life, we will face some worries, some trials, the temptation to become solely focused on what's going on in this earthly life. So, what should be the objects of our attention and focus? A heavenly perspective, God's Kingdom, its reality, and the righteousness proceeding from it to us. When we think like Jesus, we prioritize His Kingdom and His righteousness, and everything else that we need will be provided.

A new definition of "first place"

So far, we have explored focusing on God the Father, living by faith, looking at past examples of God's faithfulness, and seeking the Kingdom of God. I think it's also important to discuss Jesus' definition of greatness. Definitions are important; if you define something incorrectly, your whole approach and actions are misguided. The mind of Jesus has a completely opposite view of greatness compared to the mind of this world as highlighted in the Gospel of Mark:

Then James and John, the sons of Zebedee, came over and spoke to him. "Teacher," they said, "we want you to do us a favor." "What is your request?" he asked. They replied, "When you sit on your glorious throne, we want to sit in places of honor next to you, one on your right and the other on your left." But Jesus said to them, "You don't know what you are asking! Are you able to drink from the bitter cup of suffering I am about to drink? Are you able to be baptized with the baptism of suffering I must be baptized with?"

"Oh yes," they replied, "we are able!"

Then Jesus told them, "You will indeed drink from my bitter cup and be baptized with my baptism of suffering. But I have no right to say who will sit on my right or my left. God has prepared those places for the ones he has chosen."

When the ten other disciples heard what James and John had asked, they were indignant. So Jesus called them together and said, "You know that the rulers in this world lord it over their people, and officials flaunt their authority over those under them. But among you it will be different. Whoever wants to be a leader among you must be your servant, and whoever wants to be first among you must be the slave of everyone else. For even the Son of Man came not to be served but to serve others and to give his life as a ransom for many."

Mark 10:35-45 NLT (emphasis added)

In Biblical times, the right-hand and left-hand seats next to a ruler were considered positions of power and prominence. It meant authority. I can understand why James and John asked for them! I can also understand why the other ten disciples were mad when they heard about it—they wanted those seats too! Jesus uses this request from James and John as an opportunity to reveal His thoughts on what it means to be truly great.

Firstly, Jesus explains that *greatness means persecution*. If you don't experience persecution for your Christian beliefs from time to time, you need to ask yourself why. When we apply the Word of God and live according to what it says, some people will be offended by that, leading to mockery or unpleasant reactions. Not because we are rude or offensive (we definitely don't need any more of those kinds of Christians) but usually because we won't conform to the morals of popular culture.

Secondly, Jesus explains that *greatness means servanthood*. Until this point, His disciples had viewed leadership as being top-down where the person at the top was better than those beneath. Jesus clearly says that our thinking about what it means to be first place should be different. There is nothing wrong with desiring to be great at what we do in life. Where the problem often lies, however, is the motivation that's driving us. Jesus never condemned the desire to be great; He questioned the motive. He questioned the motive of why we desire to be great!

_____

_____

_____

_____

_____

_____

_____

Our church, ChurchLV, started in our living room. Wendy and I didn't start the church because we wanted to be famous and promote ourselves. Motivation like that would never have gotten us through the trials and challenges that were to come! Our motivation was to obey God and serve the people in our community. As we gathered 27 people in our home, we just had this sense that God would take care of the future.

Servanthood is the mindset of Jesus. Servanthood is not a low place; it's a high place. Jesus did not rebuke the disciples for desiring greatness; He redefined it for them. I want to encourage you to take on the mind of Jesus when it comes to serving others. And I am not just referring to volunteering in your local church. A servanthood mindset frames all areas of our lives. It frames our marriages, how we raise our children, how we interact with others, and how we treat our colleagues, employees, and employers.

Thirdly, Jesus explains that *greatness means giving your life away*. I accepted Jesus as my Lord and Savior in the July of 1986. My youth pastor's name was Doug. One evening, after a youth service, Doug announced that he needed people every week to help set up the chairs before a service and then pack them down again at the end of the service. I looked around and saw that nobody was responding. After a few moments, I slowly raised my hand. I was the only one who volunteered.

The ironic thing was that leading up to this event, I had been praying to God, asking Him to use me in a significant way. I was praying that I'd get to be that world-changer that my eighth-grade teacher had called me all those years prior. "Use me, God! Use me for Your glory!" To be honest, I was thinking about the platform and the microphone. But God's response was, "I've heard your prayer. Here are 250 chairs."

In that season, God was using me for His glory. He was shaping me for His glory. He was teaching me true greatness and changing my mindset of what it means to be in first place. I received an understanding in that season of setting up chairs and packing them away again. I discovered that the road of serving is what takes you to your destiny. That season removed my driving desire for a platform. It removed my need for a microphone. It removed my affirmation to be seen. Little did I know what was ahead for me in the days to come. Being great became doing whatever God had called me to do and doing it to the best of my ability, knowing it was all about others. It was about giving my life away.

The reality is that we are all giving away our lives to something or for someone. And if you want to know what or who that something or someone is, simply take a look at your priorities.

Reflection

Use the following questions to take an inventory of your life.

- Are the first things first?
- Is your focus on God the Father?
- Are you living by faith?
- Do you know what your birds and flowers are?
- Are you seeking first the Kingdom of God?
- What does greatness look like in your life right now?

Journal your responses below.

_____

_____

_____

_____

_____

_____

_____

_____

_____

_____

_____

_____

_____

_____

_____

_____

_____

_____

_____

_____

_____

_____

_____

_____

_____

_____

_____

_____

_____

_____

_____

_____

Study verses:
Matthew 6:24-34, Mark 10:35-45, Ephesians 1:22

Chapter 6

Jesus Thinks Obedience and Trust

As a pastor and preacher, I know there are certain words and topics that get an excited response from a congregation—miracles, abundance, and providence, just to name a few. However, words and topics like obedience and trust don't seem to elicit the same response! I believe the reason why we react that way is because we view God the wrong way. We may have unhealthy and incorrect mindsets when it comes to obeying and trusting God because we have had negative experiences from our own upbringing in which significant people in our lives let us down deeply.

However, living with the mind of Jesus gives us a whole new revelation of obedience and trust because even Jesus Himself said that He came to earth to obey what God the Father had purposed for His life (see John 6:38). Jesus did not obey His Father out of fear; He obeyed out of secure love. When you view God the Father the right way—as a loving Heavenly Father who desires the best for you—you will view His redirection and discipline in an entirely different way.

We think understanding; Jesus thinks obedience

The Gospel of Mark recounts one of Jesus' most well-known miracles, which I believe teaches us a new way of thinking.

By the time Jesus came ashore, a massive crowd was waiting. At the sight of them, his heart was filled with compassion, because they seemed like wandering sheep who had no shepherd. So he taught them many *wonderful* things.

Late that afternoon, his disciples said, "It's getting really late and we're here in this remote place with nothing to eat. You should send the crowds away so they can go into the surrounding villages and buy food."

But he answered them, "You give them something to eat."

"Are you sure?" they replied.

"You really want us to go buy them supper? It would cost a small fortune to feed all these thousands of hungry people."

"How many loaves of bread do you have?" he asked.

"Go and see."

After they had looked around, they came back and said, "Five—plus a couple of fish."

Then he instructed them to organize the crowd and have them sit down in groups on the grass. So they had them sit down in groups of hundreds and fifties. Then Jesus took the five loaves and two fish, gazed into heaven, and gave thanks to God. He broke the bread and the two fish and distributed them to his disciples to serve the people—*and the food was multiplied in front of their eyes!* Everyone had plenty to eat and was fully satisfied. Then the twelve disciples picked up what remained, and each of them ended up with a basket full of leftovers! Altogether, five thousand families were fed that day!

Mark 6:34-44 TPT

A major difference between the disciples' perspective and Jesus' perspective is that the disciples focus on the problems while Jesus focuses on the people. The disciples are driven by the urgent need to find solutions; Jesus is moved by compassion. Furthermore, Jesus also sees the crowds as sheep without a shepherd. Sheep need a shepherd! Why? Without a shepherd moving them forward, sheep will remain in one grazing place for too long, and they will not only eat the grass but will eat the roots. A place of abundance will turn into a place of lack, and where there was once feasting will be a famine. The shepherd is responsible for keeping the sheep grazing only long enough for what they need without consuming the source of their provision.

Too big for whom?

This passage makes it clear that it was getting late, they were in a remote place, and there was nothing to eat. The disciples come to Jesus. Notice what they say. They tell Him the problem and then tell Him what He should do about it. I personally find that funny; however, I am also guilty of doing the same thing. As if Jesus didn't already know the problem! So many of our prayers are filled with information that God already knows, but we need to allow Him to tell us what we don't know.

The reason why they tell Jesus what to do is because they believe that the problem is bigger than their resource. They are unable to solve the situation in their own strength, so they bring the problem to Jesus. Often, it's not until we come to the end of ourselves that we finally come to Jesus. We arrive at a desolate and deserted place. We enter into a wilderness that is dark with nothing to eat. And yet, this is the very place that Jesus is getting to perform a miracle. In the same way, God is getting ready to show up in your desperate circumstances and do something you have never seen before!

Jesus' response to the disciples challenges their way of thinking. He flips the script on them and tells *them* to feed the crowds. Again, the disciples explain how this is impossible because of how much this would cost. They were not thinking the way Jesus was thinking, which is made evident when Jesus then asks them to report back on what they *do* have. I wonder what you would find if you listened to Jesus' instruction to "go and see." The disciples discover five loaves of bread and some fish. What is it that you have? It may not seem like enough, but that is the point. The problem with our thinking is that we look at our resources, and we see the problem. We declare, "This problem is too big!" Jesus' question is, "Too big for whom?" Yes, it's too big for you, but it's not too big for Him!

_____

_____

_____

_____

_____

_____

Why do we struggle to obey God?

The struggle is real no matter how long you have been a follower of Jesus. We will all go through circumstances and seasons in life in which we find it difficult to obey. From my own experience, here are three reasons why I think we can struggle to obey God.

1. We look through the wrong lens.

I wear glasses and have yearly appointments with the optometrist to have my eyes checked and tested to make sure my prescription for the lenses in my glasses is still correct. I find the equipment quite fascinating; especially the machine called the phoropter. It's one of the main tools used by optometrists to determine the eyeglass numbers of the patient. Perhaps you are familiar with what happens. When I go in for my eye test, I'm instructed to sit in front of an eye chart some distance away. Different lenses are applied, and I need to say which one helps me to see the chart better. This feedback determines which lens provides the best vision.

When we view a situation through the wrong lens, we struggle to obey God. Let me put this another way. We tend to look at Jesus through the lens of our difficulties rather than looking at our difficulties through the lens of Jesus.

2. We choose understanding over obedience.

Chapter 4 explored the need to apply the Word of God and not just consume it as simply information. Information alone will lead us down a path of our own understanding; if we don't understand it, we are not going to do it. That's the way the world operates, but it does not work that way in the Kingdom of God.

Proverbs 3:5-6 says, "Trust in the Lord with all your heart; do not depend on your own understanding. Seek his will in all you do, and he will show you which path to take" (NLT). If we understood everything all the time, we would not mature in our faith, character, and relationship with God. As a father of three children, there have been many times, especially when they were little when they simply weren't developmentally mature enough to understand the reason for something.

When one of them would reach out their hand to touch a hot oven, my wife and I would quickly pick them up, move them away, and say they couldn't touch it because it was hot. It made total sense to an adult, right? But not to a 14-month-old child!

Have you ever considered that God intentionally does not give you all the information for a reason? God will allow you to mature to a place where you can have greater understanding, but we must begin with trusting in the Lord with all our heart and leaning not on our own understanding. The issue of trust leads me to the third point.

3. *Obedience requires trusting in the Lord.*

There will be many times when obeying God just does not make sense at that time. It will make sense in hindsight when we look back and see the providence of the Lord. Obedience starts with trust. God told Noah to build an ark when Noah had never seen rain before. God told Moses to hold out his staff over the Red Sea when the approaching Egyptians cornered the Israelites. God told Wendy and me to leave a successful preaching ministry to plant a church in Las Vegas. Things rarely make sense at the time. But they will as we trust and obey.

Let's go back to our main passage from the Gospel of Mark. The disciples have discovered the five loaves of bread and some fish. Jesus takes the bread and fish from them, blesses the food, and then hands the bread and fish back to the disciples. As you then know, the entire crowd is miraculously fed. It is vital to recognize that the multiplication took place in Jesus' hands, but the distribution took place in the disciples' hands. God is just looking for us to obey—to give back to Him. Worry is the result of holding on to something for which you're not responsible.

Trusting in God means transferring that thing into His hands so He can bless it, supernaturally multiply it, and then hand the miracle back to you to distribute it to others. Before we experience a miracle, we need an obedience mentality!

_____

_____

_____

_____

_____

_____

We think tomorrow; Jesus thinks today

One of the flaws of the human condition is that we often put off doing difficult things to tomorrow, so we don't have to deal with it today. Not only do we procrastinate and leave things until tomorrow, but we are also preoccupied with and worrying about tomorrow instead of focusing on the present. Do you ever find yourself sitting in a Sunday church service, but your mind is already on Monday?

So far in this chapter, we have focused primarily on obedience. One of the reasons I gave for why people often struggle to obey God is in regards to trust. I now want to expand upon this more from another angle by highlighting other aspects from the passage in Matthew 6, which features in the chapter, Jesus Thinks First Things First. In verse 34, it says, "Refuse to worry about tomorrow, but deal with each challenge that comes your way, one day at a time. Tomorrow will take care of itself" (TPT).

The natural tendency in culture today is to worry. Culture has made worry normal when biblically it should be abnormal! The word "worry" in this context is to be torn apart. Imagine having a horse tied to one wrist and another horse tied to the other wrist. Then imagine the horses running in the opposite direction. It would literally tear you apart. I know this is a graphic illustration, but this is what worry does on the inside of us. We get torn apart. We worry about our children, about our finances, about the future. We worry about the continuing impact of the COVID-19 pandemic and political unrest.

What is interesting is that Jesus doesn't say that worrying situations will not come our way. He acknowledges that there will be challenges we have to face daily. Jesus is telling us not to be controlled by worry even though there will be times that we feel the emotions of it. I want to add at this point that your emotions are valid and important. They are indicators but not dictators. We do not live in denial of how we feel, but we ensure that our declaration is in line with the mind of Jesus.

Eat, drink, and wear

In this particular passage, Jesus refers to three causes of worry: not having anything to eat, not having anything to drink, and not having anything to wear. Why are those the three things upon which Jesus focuses? I don't know about you, but I can think of many other things that I feel would cause me greater worry!

What we need to remember is Jesus' audience when He says these words. He is speaking to His disciples, who are Jews. These Jewish men had the Torah (the first five books of our Old Testament) memorized. They would have been brought up hearing the stories that were passed down from generation to generation of the time that God delivered their ancestors from slavery and led them through the wilderness. As Moses led them through the wilderness, there were many times when the people would start to grumble and complain, primarily about being hungry and thirsty. And each time, God miraculously provided for them. Furthermore, we read in Deuteronomy 29:5 that for the forty years they were in the wilderness, their clothes and sandals never wore out.

It is no coincidence that Jesus focuses on food, water, and clothing when addressing His disciples on the topic of worry. Eat, drink, wear—three words that would have been triggers for them. Psychologists say that we all have triggers. Triggers can be words, smells, sounds, certain situations that take our minds back to things that have happened in the past. What triggers your worry? It may not be the specific fears of not having anything to eat, drink, or wear, but we all have certain things that trigger us and cause us to worry about tomorrow. And all triggers of worry are connected to a central root question, which will come to light throughout the rest of this chapter.

Jesus deals with every trigger

With this in mind, let's now read the words of Jesus, again to His disciples, from this passage in the Gospel of John.

They replied, "Show us a miracle so we can see it, and then we'll believe in you. *Moses took care of our ancestors* who were fed by the miracle of manna every day in the desert, just like the Scripture says, 'He fed them with bread from heaven.' What sign will you perform for us?"

"The truth is," Jesus said, "Moses didn't give you the bread of heaven. It's my Father who offers bread that comes as a dramatic sign from heaven. The bread of God is the One who came out of heaven to give his life to feed the world."

"Then please, sir, give us this bread every day," they replied. Jesus said to them, "I am the Bread of Life. Come every day to me and you will never be hungry. Believe in me and you will never be thirsty.

John 6:30-35 TPT

Once again, the minds of the disciples are different to the mind of Jesus. They state that it was Moses who took care of their ancestors in the desert. They misunderstood the source of provision. They were looking to a natural man instead of to our supernatural God. They gave credit to a person that could be seen instead of to our unseen God.

It's at this point that Jesus says something deeply profound. He declares that He is the Bread of Life. He says that we can come to Him every day. Did you catch that? Every day. We worry about tomorrow, but Jesus focuses on today. We can come to Him every day and never need to worry about becoming hungry or thirsty tomorrow.

_____

_____

_____

_____

_____

_____

_____

Jesus is answering a deeper question that I believe we all ask on the inside during times of worry: What is going to sustain me? Our worries are related to sustenance, and Jesus is revealing that He is the person who will sustain us in all things every single day. He is our strength, power, and help.

What's important to recognize is that Jesus states that we must come to Him. There is an action required on our part. In our desperation, we often go to other things and other people in our quest to find sustenance. But when we are hungry or thirsty and consume the wrong food or drink, we can end up feeling hungrier and thirstier than we did before! We feast on social media, possessions, job promotions, and relationships, which leave us dissatisfied. There is nothing wrong with those things in and of themselves as long as it's Jesus to whom we come first. Jesus is our bread that satisfies our eternal hunger. Jesus is our water that quenches our eternal thirst. His righteousness, which never wears out, is what clothes us when we accept Him as our Lord and Savior!

His mercy and grace are sufficient for you today. As we conclude this chapter, be encouraged to bring your cares to the feet of Jesus—you do not need to take on tomorrow's troubles today. Trust that Jesus' grace is enough for today, and watch your faith grow!

Reflection

1. Make a list of all the things that are currently worrying you.

_____

_____

_____

_____

_____

_____

_____

_____

_____

_____

_____

_____

2. Can you identify a common thread in the above list? What is the common trigger or root of all the worry?

_____

_____

_____

_____

_____

3. Make a list of the things that are currently "in your hand." These things could include your job, your studies, your qualifications, your skills, your responsibilities, your relationships, your belongings, etc. How do you view what is currently in your hand? Are you being a faithful steward with those things?

_____

_____

_____

_____

_____

_____

_____

_____

_____

_____

_____

_____

_____

_____

_____

_____

_____

_____

_____

_____

4. Describe a time in your life when the Lord provided for you in unexpected ways.

_____

_____

_____

_____

_____

_____

_____

_____

_____

_____

_____

_____

_____

_____

Study verses:
John 6, Proverbs 3:6, Matthew 6:34

Chapter 7

A Strong Mind

Beloved friends, what should be our proper response to God's
marvelous mercies?
To surrender yourselves to God to be his sacred, living sacrifices.
And live in holiness, experiencing all that delights his heart.
For this becomes your genuine expression of worship.
Stop imitating the ideals and opinions of the culture around
you, but be inwardly transformed by the Holy Spirit through a total
reformation of how you think.
This will empower you to discern God's will as you live a beautiful
life, satisfying and perfect in his eyes.
God has given me grace to speak a warning about pride.
I would ask each of you to be emptied of self-promotion and not
create a false image of your importance. Instead, honestly assess
your worth by using your God-given faith as the standard of
measurement, and then you will see your true value
with an appropriate self-esteem.

Romans 12:1-3 TPT

More than a strong opinion

Do you know somebody who always has an opinion about everything? And are not scared of expressing it? Perhaps you are that person! There are some things that people either love or hate. There's no middle ground. We experience this in all cultures. In US American culture, one example is cheese, especially blue cheese—you either love it or you hate it, right? Whether it's food, sports, music, parenting methods, technology, or choice of brands, there is no shortage of strong opinions out there. We often say a person who has a strong opinion really knows their mind when it comes to that topic. They have a strong mind in that area.

Having strong opinions and knowing your mind is a good thing. Here's why: When we have a strong mind, a strong opinion, or a strong stance surrounding a topic, our resulting decisions, actions, responses, and direction flow freely. If you don't like blue cheese, you are not going to order a salad that comes with blue cheese. If you prefer the Raiders over the Patriots (as you should), it's easy to decide which game to watch. These are easy decisions because we hold strong opinions.

Sometimes, however, these strongly held opinions can get us into trouble. Have you ever been in an argument, discussion, or a situation and suddenly realized that you were wrong? But you were just too embarrassed to admit it? We often have a hard time admitting when we're wrong. There have been times when I have been halfway through an argument, have suddenly realized that the other person's point actually made more sense than my own—and yet, I either didn't admit I was wrong, or I took a while to finally confess!

Here's an example. I, Wendy, was recently in the closet. I would love to write that I was cleaning out the closet, but I was not—I was just in the closet. As I picked up an item of clothing, I was convinced that I saw a very large spider scurry along the floor. In that moment, it was my truth. My strong opinion. Now, my husband, Benny, is not only a very discerning man but also finds me highly dramatic. Not a helpful combination!

Nonetheless, I made my way downstairs to where he was working and did my best to calmly get his attention. He took one look at me, and I instantly knew that he was not fooled by my calm exterior. I clearly must have been exuding all this negative energy. Frankly, I was already mentally planning how quickly we could move out of the house in order to get it fumigated.

"What is it, Wendy?" Benny asked, raising an eyebrow, slightly amused.

At that point, I was convinced I could feel spiders crawling up my legs. "There's a spider in our closet! A really big one. I really need you to kill it and to kill it now! There's no way I can go back in there knowing there's a spider in the closet!"

Benny marched upstairs, and trying to be helpful, I offered to get the Dyson.

Benny, clearly bothered by the interruption and my drama, replied, "I don't need a Dyson; I have a foot!"

After several minutes of rummaging through the closet, he exclaimed, "Oh, I see it!" I felt relieved. Then his expression changed. "Oh, it's not a spider. That's just the wood from the floor. Let me keep looking."

It suddenly dawned on me. What if the "spider" I had "seen" was actually the wood from the floor too? I said nothing. I just let Benny rearrange and clean out the closet! It wasn't until later that night, over dinner, that I finally confessed.

"So, Benny, that spider today…" I began sheepishly.

He instantly replied, "Yeah, I know. There wasn't any spider, right?"

I had been unable to admit I was wrong as soon as I had realized it. My strongly held opinion of being unable to cohabitate with spiders prevented me from swallowing my pride. But more about pride later.

_____

_____

_____

_____

_____

_____

A strong mind is a renewed mind

Evidently, having a strong mind as a Christian means more than just having strong opinions. If we want to live a fulfilled, successful, and victorious life here on earth, and become more like Jesus, it requires more than strong opinions—we need a strong mind!

The Bible defines a strong mind as a renewed mind. If you've been a follower of Jesus and in church for a while, this term, "renewed," will be familiar to you. However, for people who are new to faith and without a church background, this can be quite confusing.

A renewed mind is a transformed mind. When we first encounter Jesus, we already think a certain way; we have strong opinions. We filter all information, interactions, and circumstances through our own perspective, which is based on our background, education, and experiences. After this all goes through those filters, we then make a decision.

Once we come to Jesus and accept Him as our Lord and Savior, those filters still matter, but they can no longer be the preeminent filter. We now have a new filter, and that filter is the Word of God. That filter is the words of Jesus. After Jesus' crucifixion and resurrection, He ushered in a new covenant upon which we now base our new way of thinking. Our minds become renewed—they are transformed.

So, it's no longer just about me having a strong opinion; as a follower of Jesus, I now have to take even my most strongly held beliefs—the ones I grew up with, the ones my family had, the ones society taught me—and line them up against the teachings of Jesus. I must ask myself: "Do my strong opinions line up with the Word of God or not?" This is the responsibility of all followers of Jesus in order to grow in spiritual maturity.

Christianity is a relationship

In light of this, Paul's words in Romans 12:1-3 are so important—not just for the Roman church to whom he was originally writing, but also to all churches and believers. Many people want to just wrap up Christianity with other religions and boil it all down to simply a set of ethical standards—a list of dos and don'ts. But that's not what Christianity is.

Christianity is a relationship! God did not create us to be robots. He created us for relationship. We are not like any other religion. Yes, we have boundaries. Yes, there are principles by which we live. Yes, there are moral absolutes in our lives. However, the Apostle Paul exhorts us to think higher, live higher, and experience a relationship with Jesus, and not reduce Christianity down to a list of rules to follow. We need to remember that God, the creator of all things, who has no beginning and no end, who is all-powerful and all-knowing, desires a relationship with us.

God can handle our hard questions

My parents were pastors. During my younger years, I was always that child that raised my hand in the middle of a Sunday School lesson—not to give an answer but, rather, to ask yet another question about something I did not understand or agree with. I was always asking the hard questions. I'm sure it drove the poor teachers crazy. In fact, they even contacted my parents a few times to express their concerns!

God is not intimidated by your questions, even though my teachers were. He's not intimidated by the times you cry out, "Why, God?" He's not intimidated by you taking your strongly held beliefs and saying, "God, I don't understand! This is the way I feel and think. This is the way I grew up. This is my history. This is how I've been taught to think my entire life. But yet, I read your Word, and what I think does not line up with what your Word says! And I'm having a hard time letting go!"

In my own life, I have recently been through a season in which the Holy Spirit has lovingly, yet firmly, challenged some strongly held beliefs that I didn't even realize I had. The COVID-19 pandemic certainly was and continues to be a great revealer of our mindsets and opinions. To be honest, it was a struggle to allow the Holy Spirit to renew and transform my thinking in some areas. However, I took great comfort in the fact that God is not intimidated by my raw emotions and questions.

There have also been challenging times in which both Benny and I continually asked the "why?" question. In fact, I asked it daily for a season! "Why is this happening, God? Why don't you seem to be changing anything? Why did you allow this to happen? I don't understand! I did not sign up for this!" Can you relate? Thank God that He is not intimidated by our souls and the darkness or the questions. He is aware and is still in control. He does not always give me the answers I may be looking for, but He is always there.

There is a verse in the Bible, which I particularly love. It says, "'Come now, and let us reason together,' says the Lord" (Isaiah 1:18 NKJV). God does not ask us to suspend our intellect. He wants us to engage intellectually with Him. He desires a relationship with us!

_____

_____

_____

_____

_____

_____

A living sacrifice

The Apostle Paul pleads with the Roman church to give their bodies to God. In other words, we are told to give all of ourselves to the Lord daily. Not just on a Sunday when we turn up at church. Daily. When we are at home with our families, when we are with our spouses or children, when we are at the office or in the classroom, when we are at the check-out paying for groceries, when we are out driving in our cars. We are told to give all of ourselves because of all He has done for us. We are to be a living and holy sacrifice.

It is important to understand that this would have been provoking language to the church to whom Paul was writing because they would have grown up with animal sacrifices. Once the animal had been sacrificed, the act was complete. However, Paul now takes things to a new level, calling us to be living sacrifices. Not just a one-off thing, but a lifestyle thing! That means that every part of us—everything we do and everything we say—is an act of worship.

I wonder what would happen if we saw every aspect of our lives as worship. I believe it would reframe how we actually do life. Let me explain using myself as the example: I wonder if I, Wendy, saw exercise and eating healthily as worship to God that it would change my mindset about what I'm putting into my body. I wonder if I, Wendy, saw the way I handle my finances as worship to God that it would cause me to budget, spend, and save differently. I wonder if I, Wendy, saw how I used my time and invested my energy as worship to God that it would change my priorities and schedule. I'm sure you're getting where I am going with this! This is not about condemnation but, rather, having a revelation that God is not just after portions of your life. He wants all of you!

Holy means being set apart. What does the phrase "set apart" mean to you? For some, it takes them back to a time when women had to wear dresses to church and men had to wear three-piece suits. It was about looking different externally. However, Paul makes it clear that being set apart is spiritual, not physical. As followers of Jesus, we are special and different from the world around us. Imagine seeing ourselves the way He sees us. Knowing that we are set apart encourages and empowers us to live a life of worship. This is intelligent and thoughtful worship. It's a life that says, "Lord, every aspect of my life is worship for all you have done for me."

Let God

There is a reason why this passage of scripture tells us not to copy the behavior and customs of this world. The ways of this world are all about trying to live life in our own strength and understanding. The behaviors and customs of this world don't enable us to let God have His way. Are you currently unhappy in your marriage? Let God! Are you currently struggling with parenting your children? Let God! Are you currently experiencing a hard work situation? Let God! Whatever it may be, we can be so tempted to react according to the behavior and customs of this world rather than letting God reframe our response.

The word "transform" is used sparingly throughout the entire Bible. It is used in reference to the transfiguration of Jesus, in which His entire appearance is transformed:

> Now after six days Jesus took Peter, James, and John his
> brother, led them up on a high mountain by themselves; and He
> was transfigured before them. His face shone like the sun, and His
> clothes became as white as the light.

> Matthew 17:1-2 NLT

This is the same way Paul uses the powerful word of transformation in Romans chapter 12. It literally means being changed from one thing into another. It's the process of a caterpillar going into a cocoon and then coming out as a butterfly. As our minds are renewed, we are transformed, and our transformation will shine brightly to those around us. It is not instantaneous. It is an ongoing process that repeats itself throughout our entire walk with Jesus on this side of eternity. You are constantly being transformed into the image of Jesus. Your mind is constantly being renewed and transformed into the mind of Jesus! As soon as you get a breakthrough in one area, the Holy Spirit starts speaking to you about the next, and about the next, and about the next! Why is this so important? Because it keeps us grounded and steeped in humility (remember how I mentioned earlier that I would bring up pride?).

For a long time, I was confused by what seems like a bizarre shift from Romans 12:1-2 to Romans 12:3. Paul goes from beautifully writing about transformation, renewing the mind, and worship, then shifts gears, almost jarringly, to address and warn us about pride. This just didn't initially make sense to me, and I couldn't make the connection when I was first studying these verses. Over time, it clicked. These verses actually do go together perfectly. Let me explain why.

Unfortunately, we have all encountered judgmental and self-righteous Christians. I'm sure some faces are appearing in your mind as you read this. Do you know how we can become judgmental and self-righteous? By abdicating the process of transformation. I started this chapter by stating that if we want a victorious, fulfilled, and successful walk with Jesus, it will take a strong mind, and a strong mind is a transformed mind. But you don't have to stay in the process of transformation. You can stop at any time! And when we stop the process of transformation, we allow pride, self-importance, and self-righteousness to rule because it is only when we stay in the process of transformation that we allow the Holy Spirit to challenge the strongly held beliefs and opinions in our lives and remain grounded in humility.

_____

_____

_____

_____

_____

_____

_____

So, how do we cultivate a strong mind?

Listen to the Holy Spirit

It is not enough to simply reduce an encounter with the Holy Spirit to a weekly event in a church building. We must continually be inviting the

Holy Spirit into our transformation process and responding to Him when He speaks to us.

Meanwhile, the boy Samuel served the Lord by assisting Eli. Now in those days messages from the Lord were very rare, and visions were quite uncommon.

One night Eli, who was almost blind by now, had gone to bed. The lamp of God had not yet gone out, and Samuel was sleeping in the Tabernacle near the Ark of God. Suddenly the Lord called out, "Samuel!"

"Yes?" Samuel replied. "What is it?" He got up and ran to Eli. "Here I am. Did you call me?"

"I didn't call you," Eli replied. "Go back to bed." So he did.

Then the Lord called out again, "Samuel!"

Again Samuel got up and went to Eli. "Here I am. Did you call me?" "I didn't call you, my son," Eli said. "Go back to bed."

Samuel did not yet know the Lord because he had never had a message from the Lord before.

So the Lord called a third time, and once more Samuel got up and went to Eli. "Here I am. Did you call me?"

Then Eli realized it was the Lord who was calling the boy. So he said to Samuel, "Go and lie down again, and if someone calls again, say, 'Speak, Lord, your servant is listening.'" So Samuel went back to bed.

And the Lord came and called as before, "Samuel! Samuel!"

And Samuel replied, "Speak, your servant is listening."

1 Samuel 3:1-10 NLT

The Holy Spirit is speaking to us every day. Just like Samuel had a hard time discerning the voice of God, so do we. What does the voice of the Holy Spirit sound like at first? Usually, that person that was instrumental in your life in bringing you closer to Jesus: your grandfather, your mother, a pastor. It's like you hear their voice in your head or heart. They were the first spokesperson of God into your life, and so you can usually recognize the same tone when you hear the voice of the Holy Spirit talking to you. It will always line up with the Bible.

Expose yourself to how Jesus thinks about it

There is no way that we can challenge strongly held opinions and beliefs and have a strong mind that is based on the Word of God if we do not know what the Bible says about different topics! We need to study the words of Jesus in order to think like Him. What does Jesus say? We live in an era in which so many Christians are debating issues that are not of primary importance. We must go back to focusing on what Jesus said and choosing to align our thinking with those words. Get in a small group and study a book of the Bible, continue your education by taking some courses online, ask your group leader or pastor for some good material to learn more about Jesus and the Word of God.

Embrace Jesus' thoughts

Humans are stubborn creatures, not naturally prone to easily changing their minds. You don't go from having a strongly held belief and, all of a sudden, read the Bible, discover you are wrong, snap your fingers, and change your mind! No! That just doesn't happen. We must practice this new way of thinking. At first, it feels awkward and foreign, but we must learn to embrace these new thoughts about ourselves and others. Our minds grow stronger as we keep moving forward, putting into practice the words of Jesus.

Think Like Jesus every day

As we conclude this journey together, remember that it is God's grace that enables you to live this out. Thinking like Jesus results in a changed life. May you experience transformation from the inside-out as you commit to putting on the mind of Jesus. May you never be the same again.

Reflection

1. Have any of your strongly held opinions been challenged recently?
Describe what took place. What was the outcome?

_____

_____

_____

_____

_____

_____

_____

_____

2. What topics or situations cause you to become judgmental of those
with different opinions? Why do you think that is?

_____

_____

_____

_____

_____

_____

_____

_____

3. Ask the Holy Spirit to reveal the unhelpful filters that currently distort your perspective. Write down what you sense the Holy Spirit saying to you.

_____

_____

_____

_____

_____

_____

_____

4. How do you feel about your everyday life being a continual sacrifice of worship? What area of your life could be transformed if you approached it with this view?

_____

_____

_____

_____

_____

5. List one practical step you can take this week to grow more in your understanding of the Bible.

_____

_____

_____

_____

_____

Study verses:
Romans 12:1-3, Matthew 17:1-2, 1 Samuel 3:1-10

Notes:

_____

_____

_____

_____

_____

_____

_____

_____

_____

_____

_____

_____

_____

_____

_____

_____

_____

_____

_____

Acknowledgments

Thank you, Celina Mina, for taking a vision and giving it life.

Thank you, Pastor Michael El-Takrori, for your contribution to the content and our community. You and Gia make this journey of faith so worth it.

Thank you, Randy Powell, for keeping us sane in all of life's ups and downs.

To our beloved staff, church family, and friends—we love you. Thank you for building an incomparable community of faith with us.

The best is yet to come.

ABOUT THE AUTHORS

BENNY & WENDY PEREZ

Pastors Benny and Wendy Perez are dynamic communicators with a passion to see people encounter Jesus. Together, they pastor ChurchLV in Las Vegas, Nevada. ChurchLV is a multi-ethnic and multi-generational church that exists to help lead people to encounter new life in Jesus. Both Benny and Wendy serve on the leadership team of the Association of Related Churches (ARC) and the Champions Network. Benny and Wendy are sought-after international speakers and currently reside in Henderson, Nevada, along with their three children, BJ, Bella, and Benaiah.

For inquiries to have Benny or Wendy speak
please contact us via BennyPerez.com

https://bennyperez.com

FAITHFUL.PLACE

Follow Wendy on Faithful

EMPOWERING WOMEN TO PREACH,
LEAD & BE THEMSELVES
UNAPOLOGETICALLY

https://faithful.place/users/iheartwendy

✝ CHURCHLV

ChurchLV is a non-denominational Christian Church in the Las Vegas
Valley, with a mission to lead people to encounter new life in Jesus.
ChurchLV is led by Benny and Wendy Perez who have devoted their life
to ministry and have been able to travel the world speaking at numerous
Christian Churches across the nation. The first Christian Church in the
Las Vegas Valley was believed to be built in 1857 with 20 members and
in similar fashion Benny and Wendy Perez hosted Church Services with
27 members at their home in 2002.

CHURCHLV.COM

Previous Books

BUILT:
Seven Principles of Leaders
Who Beat the Odds, Escape
Average, And Make a Lasting
Impact

Foreword by Tommy Barnett

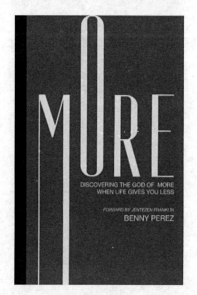

MORE:
Discovering the God of More
When Life Gives You Less

Foreword by Jentezen Franklin

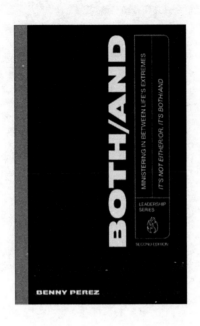

BOTH/AND:
Ministering In Between
Life's Extremes, A Church
Leaders Guide to Creating a
"Both And" Culture in Your
Church